E. B. Pusey

The Responsibility of Intellect in Matters of Faith

A sermon, preached before the University of Oxford, on Advent Sunday, 1872. With an appendix on Bishop Moberly's strictures on the warning clauses of the Athanasian Creed

E. B. Pusey

The Responsibility of Intellect in Matters of Faith
A sermon, preached before the University of Oxford, on Advent Sunday, 1872. With an appendix on Bishop Moberly's strictures on the warning clauses of the Athanasian Creed

ISBN/EAN: 9783744750875

Printed in Europe, USA, Canada, Australia, Japan

Cover: Foto ©Lupo / pixelio.de

More available books at **www.hansebooks.com**

The Responsibility of Intellect in Matters of Faith:

A SERMON,

PREACHED BEFORE THE UNIVERSITY OF OXFORD,

ON ADVENT SUNDAY, 1872.

With an Appendix

ON BISHOP MOBERLY'S STRICTURES ON THE WARNING CLAUSES OF THE ATHANASIAN CREED.

BY

E. B. PUSEY, D.D.

REGIUS PROFESSOR OF HEBREW, AND CANON OF CHRIST CHURCH.

SOLD BY
JAMES PARKER & CO., OXFORD,
AND 377, STRAND, LONDON:
RIVINGTONS, WATERLOO PLACE, LONDON,
HIGH STREET, OXFORD, AND TRINITY STREET, CAMBRIDGE.
1873.

THE RESPONSIBILITY OF INTELLECT IN MATTERS OF FAITH.

" He that rejecteth Me, and receiveth not My words, hath one that judgeth him: the word that I have spoken, the same shall judge him in the last day."—S. JOHN xii. 48.

GOD, in this close of the expiring year, preaches death, at once in the world and in the Church, to the eye of sight and to the eye of faith, by sights of nature and the tempered beauty of its calm decay, by the enforced thought of those who, in this little division of our being, have been parted from us and have said, each in his turn, to us, "Thou too must follow," or by Advent's trumpet-call, "Prepare to meet thy God[1]." So are the thoughts of death impressed upon the mind, that even those who are most busied with the world's shifting scenes, linger, at least for one little day, upon the memories of the past rather than on thoughts of the future, reviewing, who of those who have, in whatever province, left some little

[1] Amos iv. 12.

impress of their work upon their own generation, have in this past year sunk out of sight, to be seen by us here no more.

And with the thought of death comes almost spontaneously the thought of judgment. The Apostle's words, "It is appointed unto all men once to die, and after that the judgment [2]," repeat authoritatively what, however suppressed for a time, is almost inextinguishably written in the human heart. The heathen too knew of that endless separation, whereby each should go to his own place, each should end in that unending end, for which all his life was a preparation. They who hated the doctrine, and would, if they could, extirpate it, bear witness to its hold upon the hearts of men. "Now," says the Atheist Lucretius [3], "there is no way or power of resisting, since in death we have to fear eternal pains." "Forth must be driven headlong from its very base the fear of Acheron, which troubles in its inmost core the life of man, suffusing all things with the dark hue of death, and leaves no pleasure unalloyed and pure [4]." "Rightly," says Celsus [5],

---

[2] Heb. ix. 27.

[3] "If men saw any certain end of sufferings, they might in some way resist religions and the threats of prophesiers; now," &c. De Rer. Nat. i. 107—111.

[4] Ib. iii. 37—40.

[5] In Orig. c. Cels. n. 49, pp. 777, 778, ed. De la Rue. Other passages are collected in the *Christian Remembrancer*, 1863, t. xlv. pp. 464 sqq.

when writing against the resurrection of the body, "Rightly at least do they [the Christians] think this, that they who have lived well shall be in bliss, but the wicked shall wholly dwell with everlasting suffering. And from this doctrine neither should they nor any other among men ever depart." Human nature too has a test of truth,—that which has been "always, every where, and by all" believed, and the voice of all is the voice of the secret teaching of God in the hearts of all. Nay, Plato, but that he speaks as a polytheist, would appeal to you as Solomon[6]: "This" [severance of the good and bad] "is the judgment of the gods, O young man who deemest that thou art disregarded by them, that the worser going to the worser souls, the better to the better, in life and in all deaths, suffer and do what is meet that like should do to like. This judgment of the gods, neither thou nor any other unfortunate shall boast that he has escaped."

Nay, this voice of nature unbelief has not been able to quench in itself. "If you abuse your reason," said Diderot to his soul, "you will be unhappy, not in this life only, but after death in hell." "And who told you," the soul answers, "that there is a hell?" "If you have but a

[6] De Legg., x. p. 904. The preceding context is: "The soul, when, through its own will and strong influence it partakes of greater evil or virtue, if, united with Divine virtue, it becomes remarkably such, is transferred to a place wholly holy; if contrariwise, it passes its life contrariwise."

doubt," he rejoins, "you ought to act as if there was one." "And if I am sure that there is none?" "I defy you to it." Voltaire, cynic as to all belief, was cynical too to those who were certain as to their unbelief. "Happy are you," said he to one who believed that he had discovered the certainty of the non-existence of hell, "most happy are you. I am far from arriving at it[7]."

And not for great crimes only, as men call great, not for crimes of passion against man only, but for selfish greed [8], for secret unknown sins [9], for rebellion against God also [1], did men even in heathenism tremble at a judgment to come and eternal punishment. The men of Nineveh will rise up to judgment against us, if we fear not.

Of that awful subject, I would now speak of one aspect only; how by God's word, it will embrace our whole selves, not in regard only to the moral

---

[7] Both are cited by Nicolas, "Études Philosophiques," c. 8, t. ii. 462.

[8] "Aut qui divitiis soli incubuere repertis, Nec partem posuere suis; quæ maxima turba est." Æn. vi. 610, 611.

[9] "Quæ quis apud superos, furto lætatus inani, Distulit in seram commissa piacula mortem." Ib. 568, 569.

[1] Evidenced in the Titans, the pride of Salmoneus, and in the line put in the mouth of Theseus: "Sedet, æternumque sedebit, Infelix Theseus; Phlegyasque miserrimus omnes Admonet, et magna testatur voce per umbras, 'Discite justitiam moniti, et non temnere divos.'" Ib. 617—620. Virgil's statement may be the more taken as expressing the popular belief, since he could not resist hinting that he believed nothing of all which he had described. Ib. 894—899. Comp. the Lucretian lines, Georg. ii. 490—492.

law, written or unwritten save by the Spirit of God on the hearts of men, but our whole relation to Almighty God, how we receive His declarations about Himself, as well as how we act towards them when we have received them.

And this I do the rather, because, while with some of you, my sons, in the full exuberance of early life, a main trial is, how you will keep the body subdued to the mind, with others it is principally, how you will keep and order the mind itself. You would shrink from the naked impiety of those of old who said, " Our lips are our own ; who is Lord over us[2]?" But you are tempted to the beginning of a course, which ends in the same result. Principles are afloat all around you, which, under the name or guise of independence of thought, carried out sometimes with a reckless consistency, more often with inconsistency shrinking from its terrible results, develope into a would-be independence of *Him* Who endowed you with your powers of mind, from Whom you have all which you are or can be, to Whom you are responsible for your use of all, and will have to give account of the use which you have made of all—Almighty God.

It is tacitly assumed, that intellect is a safe and unbiassed guide; that its determinations, though not infallible, are sure and unblamable; that, if any implicitly follow it,—as a Pagan philosopher

[2] Ps. xii. 4.

might follow it, apart from any grace of God or prayer for His illumining, nay abstracting oneself for the time from the light of the Gospel,—its conclusions, although in different minds naturally contradictory and self-destructive, are necessarily right for each; that, in the things of God too, what is newest is right, what is old is superannuated and wrong, forgetting that the truths of God are eternally new as Himself, being a transcript of a portion of His unchangeable wisdom. Anyhow, men will have it, that no responsibility is incurred, be the result of any process of reasoning what it may, any more than in a proposition of mathematics; that there is no right or wrong about it; in a word, that if a person thinks he is pursuing truth, though he be more anxious to have truth on his side, than to be on the side of truth, conscience and Almighty God have no voice in the matter. The thought that each shall have to give account for his "opinions" (as people call them), or the process by which he arrived at them, seems to them as strange an imagination, as if the subject-matter were some proposition of pure mathematics.

Contrariwise, I would point out to you the responsibility of intellect; that it, as well as every other good gift of God, is capable of being abused; that, as "the corruption of the best is the worst," so the perversion of intellect has a melancholy pre-eminence of evil, as, in actual madness, the sight of a mind dethroned has a sorrowfulness beyond any guiltless sorrow; that, not speaking now of hereditary error, human intellect is liable to be influenced by every wave and eddy of human passion; that the darkness of bribed or misguided or perverted intellect is the more perilous because it *is* our guide which we trust, a darkness irremediable, unless it be again illumined by light from on high. "If the light that is *in* thee be darkness, how great is that darkness[3]!"

Intellect has, it is plain, many trials. There is not a sin or crime of our lower nature which it does not aggravate, or in aid of which it is not abused. There is not a spiritual sin, of which it is not the instrument or centre. There is nothing so debased to which, in the service of passion, it will not stoop; no vastness of evil which it will not conceive and animate. It invents ways by which to teach or incite our lower nature to offend against the laws of our nature. It will devise evil, from which our lower fellow-creatures, following blindly the laws of their limited capacities, are exempt. It conceives and effectuates those gigantic crimes at which the world grows pale. All the vices of our nature are puny and dwarfed without it. It guides to deeper evil each varied passion of our fallen nature. It severs off the seducer from the coarse and vulgar profligate; low cunning from common-place cheating; sophistry from

---

[3] S. Matt. vi. 23.

naked untruth; subtle revenge from brute anger. The worst title which we could give, to brand an action of cruelty, or revenge, or malice, or barbarity, or sensuality, would be to call it "refined," "subtle;" meaning that intellect was more than usually abused to the service of man's lower passions. "Did you never observe," asks Plato [4], "the narrow intellect flashing from the keen eye of a clever rogue, how clearly his paltry soul sees the way to his end; he is the reverse of blind, but his keen sight is taken into the service of evil, and he is dangerous in proportion to his intelligence?"

Abused intellect makes proverbs of Balaam or Ahithophel, or Jonadab, or Simon Magus. No world-wide evil ever existed without it. The scourges of mankind fell not like mere avalanches, but wielded through it their widely desolating might. If we would describe an almost superhuman abuse of intellect to evil, we call it by the name of that being of tremendous subtlety of talent, the fallen archangel, and term it "devilish." The massacre of St. Bartholomew bears witness to the wonderful talent as well as the terrible wickedness of its author, Catherine of Medicis. The rent of East and West for all these centuries [5]

---

[4] Repub. vii. p. 519; t. ii. p. 352, Jowett's Transl.

[5] The schism became irreconcilable through the conquest of Constantinople by the Crusaders. Fleuri, Discours 6, sur l'Hist. Eccl. n. 5, t. 11, p. xv.

attests the Satanic ability, wherewith Photius, conscious as he must have been of the weakness of the other grounds of quarrel, cast into the scale the allegation of heresy against our Western formula, "Filioque," although, with his vast reading, he could scarce be ignorant that it was also the language of other Greek fathers [6], and specially of the most powerful defender of the faith among themselves, recognized as such by two general Councils, S. Cyril of Alexandria [7].

But since, through the whole range of human crime and sin, the abuse of intellect has its distinct and powerful sway, and ignorance and stupidity, if not self-caused, seem to human justice also a mitigation of participated guilt, and contrariwise, clear intellect is, by universal consent, held to be an aggravation of human crime, how comes it to be assumed that, when brought face to face with Almighty God, intellect has no trial, but that, let intellect treat His revelation how it will,

---

[6] As S. Epiphanius, "The Holy Ghost is of the substance of the Father and the Son." Ancorat. c. 7; and Theodorus of Tarsus, our seventh Archbishop of Canterbury, in the hope of whose coming the VIth General Council was delayed (Ep. Agathon. in Baronius, A. 680, iv., and the Roman Synodal letter, where he is called "the great Archbishop and philosopher of the Isle of Britain." Conc. Const. Act. iv.; Ep. ii.; T. Conc. vii. 714), in the Confession of the Council of Hatfield, Sept. 17, A.D. 680. See Rev. G. Williams's Essay 8, on "The Church and the Age," p. 236, and other fathers vindicated in Petav. de Trin. vii. 3, pp. 370 sqq.

[7] See Note A at the end, p. 55.

let it reject, rebel, pare away, distort, ridicule, blaspheme it, how it may; let it substitute, if it will, some worship of nature or of itself, for the living God, man is blameless, because it is matter of intellect? If man is hurried away by passions of his lower nature to break God's laws, he is allowed to be (as he is) guilty; if, without passion, he show contempt to God Himself, he is to be held innocent! Heat of passion is held to be an extenuation of deeds of violence, because a man is less master of himself. It shocks our nature the more, if they be done in cold blood, as men say. Cold dispassionate judgments, if directed against Almighty God and His truth, are matter of self-praise. What ground can be given for these uneven measures, but that, alas! men are judges in their own cause?

In a cause which is not our own, we can judge rightly. Take the whole history of the Jews before the Captivity! True, that our moral nature comes to our aid, and, let men disbelieve of God's revelation by Moses as they will, our moral nature cannot but revolt at the moral abominations or unnatural cruelties of the nature-worships of Baal and Moloch and the calves, "the sin whereby Jeroboam made Israel to sin." Nay, not as to those grosser irreligions only, but in contrast with every form of Pagan error, not in Christianity alone, but wherever the derived heresy of Mohammedanism prevails, the whole world attests the truth of God's revelation of Himself, " Hear, O Israel, the Lord our God is one Lord [8]; " all attest the righteousness of that first commandment of God, " Thou shalt have no other gods beside Me [9]." All those irreligions, human nature attests, were errors, and those who invented, gilded, propagated them, were in antagonism to truth, known or unknown, the makers or disciples of vanities and lies, misleaders or misled. Human intellect now mostly judges rightly as to the conflict of all those centuries between the worship of nature, so marvellously contrived by human intellect to enlist on its side our human passions, our sense of the grandeur of the operations of nature, or often our perception of beauty, and the adoring love of Almighty God. Theism, Pantheism and Atheism divide now the intellectual world which will not receive the Gospel or to which it is unknown: Polytheism, which held bound the intellect of antiquity, although a natural offshoot of Pantheism, is out of favour.

Modern intellect, whatever licence it may take in criticizing the Prophets of God, will allow at least that they were in the right in their upbraidings of the revolting, degrading nature-worships of Phœnicia and Egypt. Even those, to whom S. Paul does not speak with authority, would concur in his judgment as to the " undistinguishing mind [1]," to which he says that those who " willed not to retain

[8] Deut. vi. 4. [9] Exod. xx. 3. [1] Rom. i. 28.

God in their knowledge," were abandoned, and as to the frightful consequences of its perversion.

Even in Christianity men can see the perversions of intellect, where, as in the rigidness of Novatianism or the Montanism of Tertullian, the error was unamiable. It can see that the grand strong fiery energetic intellect of Tertullian was warped by a self-confiding zeal which had too little love. But then it grants, or sets out with a presumption, that the perception of truth may be injured by deficiency in some moral quality, the want of love. The heart, it is admitted, may pervert the head. We see it every day in things of this life.

Again, in things of this world too, in every department of human knowledge, in every practical business of this life, intellect is perverted through vain-glory. "I did not rise at four," said one[2] whose name stands almost as a proverb for his paradoxes in criticism and his contempt of evidence, "to think like the rest of mankind." Truth is a sacred thing, because it is a reflection of God. Whoso seeks it not for its own sake, will never find it. All the great discoverers in science, all the benefactors of mankind, have practically sought truth, with no thought of themselves, but of it alone. Much more they who desire to behold

---

[2] The P. Hardouin, "Nouv. Dict. Historique." When he did think "like the rest of mankind," he was, by his learning and labour, of lasting service to mankind.

the God of truth and see His ways. "How can ye believe," our Blessed Lord asks, as of a thing inconceivable, " which receive honour one of another, and seek not the honour which cometh of God only[3]." "Among the chief rulers also," S. John relates, " many believed on Him, but because of the Pharisees they did not confess Him, lest they should be put out of the synagogue; for they loved the praise of men more than the praise of God[4]." Dread of shame before man made them suppress the belief, which for the time they had. They had seen Jesus: they had heard His words of attractive sweetness and might and truth; they had heard the words of Him Who spake as " never man spake;" they had seen His works, such as man could not do, " unless God were with him." Their intellect was convinced. What hindered their avowing their belief, stifled it, probably extinguished it? Alas! probably one of the most common of human infirmities,—human respect. They could not bear to be esteemed less faithful to Moses than others their equals, to be disciples of a Galilean, to forfeit the esteem wherein they were held as teachers of the law, to be cast out by their fellow-men. Was their smouldering faith, which they suppressed for fear of their compeers, while these said, " See ye that we avail nothing? behold the world is gone after Him," fanned into new life by the Crucifixion, that they

[3] S. John v. 44.   [4] S. John xii. 42, 43.

who shrank from owning Jesus, the worker of miracles, the admired and followed by the people, were among those who worshipped the Crucified? If not, then they who had once believed in Himself were among those who persecuted Him in His members and compelled them to blaspheme Him in Whom they had once believed. And yet that mental fault through which they suppressed the convictions of their intellect, is so common a fault, that a profound observer of our nature says[5], "there is scarce any one who doth not desire human glory;" nay, "vain-glory often glories more vainly of the very contempt of vain-glory; for it doth not contemn when it glorieth, and so it is no longer contempt of vain-glory[6]." And yet vain-glory all must own to be a fault. Its name is framed to stamp it as a fault. Heathenism too, while it idolized love of glory, framed the term which condemns it.

Heathenism again could own that central spring of all spiritual sin, pride, to be, in some shapes and forms a fault. It was, it is thought, *the* sin which changed Satan from one of the Cherubim arrayed with grace, into an apostate spirit. Satan, who knew the power of the temptation on himself, essayed it on our first parents. Through their fall they transmitted it as a central infirmity of our race.

Man cannot, of course, admit that pride is, in

[5] S. Aug. in Ps. i.   [6] Conf. x. 38, p. 219, Oxf. Tr.

his own case or in that of his compeers, the cause of his unbelief or misbelief. It would be to condemn themselves. No one altogether proud would think himself proud, even as no humble man could think himself humble. But look back then to the origin of Christianity. None probably has any sympathy with the Pharisee, who " counted himself that he was righteous and despised others." Yet this was the centre of the Jews' rejection of the Gospel, as is developed by S. Paul; " going about to establish their own righteousness, they submitted themselves not to the righteousness of God[7]." They who held themselves " not to be sinners from the Gentiles[8]," what need had they of a Redeemer ? " They that are whole need not a physician," our Lord said to them, " but they that are sick. I came not to call the righteous, but sinners to repentance[9]." Even in S. Augustine's time many heathen would not be converted, on the ground that, since they led good lives, they had no need of Christ[1].

[7] Rom. x. 3.   [8] Gal. ii. 15.   [9] S. Luke v. 31, 32.

[1] " Many glory in their works, and you find many heathen who on that ground are unwilling to become Christians, because they are, as it were, self-sufficing with their good life. He says, ' You must live well; what will Christ teach me ? To live well ? I live well already. For what have I need of Christ ? I commit no homicide, no theft, no rapine ; I covet not goods of others; I am defiled by no adultery. Let any thing blameworthy be found in my life, and he who shall find fault in me make me a Christian.'" In Ps. xxxi.; Enarr. II. n. 2, Opp. iv. 171.

In the light of the history of Christianity, we, even apart from our faith, can discern the pride of those who superciliously dismissed it as unworthy of their notice. On the one side was the Carpenter and His disciples, the fishermen, the tax-gatherer and the tent-maker. On the other, the great world-subduing empire, its marvellous political sagacity, its centuries of glory, and the hereditary wisdom of those wonderful creations of God, those keen penetrating intellects of Greece which still form and sharpen our own intellects. The pride of intellect or power had temptations which we see only as in a picture, yet unconquerable save by the overpowering grace of God. But how do we look back upon it? Christian history alone embalms the lifeless memories of Pilate who asked, " What is truth [2]?" or of Gallio who " cared for none of these things [3];" or of the Epicurean or Stoic philosophers, who counted Paul " a babbler [4];" or of the philosophers of Mars' hill, who mocked at the resurrection of Jesus; or of Festus, who held that it was a small matter that " one Jesus, who was dead, Paul affirmed to be alive [5]." Or in these days in which free inquiry is idolized, what think we of the terms, wherewith Heathen intellect dismissed the claims before which the intellect of the world has bowed? Looking at the Gospel for the moment, as a power

[2] S. John xviii. 38. [3] Acts xviii. 17.
[4] Acts xvii. 18. [5] Acts xxv. 19.

transforming mankind, what can we think of such terms as these, employed to designate and dismiss it, "folly [6]," "vain folly," "vanity," "empty vanity," "execrable vanity," "blind error," "pernicious error," "vain and mad superstition," "old wives' superstitions" or "doctrines" or "fables" or "inventions and absurdities," "womanly superstition," "puerile phrenzies" or "follies," "things ridiculous," "foolish trifles," "unreasonable belief," "presumption," "credulity," "phrenzy?" Or what bias was it to praise "the just man, tenacious of his purpose, whose firm-poised soul no tyrant's threatening mien should shake, nor popular zeal enjoining things perverse [7]," and yet condemn for "inflexible obstinacy which ought to be punished [8]," "rash desperation [9]," "phrenzy," those who, rather than curse [1] or deny their Saviour, accounted all suffering joy, and by three centuries of endurance conquered the world which would exterminate [2] them. Did those who

[6] See the authorities in Kortholt de Cal. Pag. c. 10, and thence in Tertull. de test. an., p. 136, n. s., Oxf. Tr.

[7] Hor. Carm. ii. 3, init.

[8] Plin. Ep. ad Traj.

[9] See in Kortholt in Plin. et Traj. Epp. p. 57, and de Cal. Pag. c. 11; also in Tertull. Apol. n. 27, p. 67, n. s., Oxf. Tr.; de Spect. n. 1, p. 188, n. f. Ib.

[1] To "curse Christ" was required in addition to the idolatrous sacrifices, as proof that the accused were no longer Christians. Plin. l. c.

[2] Nomine Christianorum deleto, "superstitione Christi ubique deleta." Inscr. Diocletian. in Hisp. ap. Baron. Ann. 302, ix.

used these terms leave their intellect free to appreciate that "power of God unto salvation," which they kept at a distance and condemned unheard? Had not "the wisdom of this world" been wiser, if it had been humbler and had listened instead of scoffing? But is there then no pride, whensoever intellect dismisses beforehand the claims of the Creator to be heard by His creature, because it is too much occupied with the things of this world, its politics, its passionate pursuit of material prosperity, its scientific investigation of the works of God, Whom it ignores? Is there no pride in regarding the Creator as a disturbing force to the laws of His creation, or in dismissing the proofs which He has given of His Being, His Providence, His revelation of Himself, because He cannot be discerned by our senses or beheld by human vision, until in the beatific vision it be enabled by Himself to behold Himself.

Then strict, unwavering, unwarped justice, what a grace it is! Heathenism mourned that, after the golden age of man's innocence, justice left the earth, shining only thenceforth upon it from her native skies. It deified the three whom it knew of by tradition, as judges of singular uprightness, and made them judges of each soul of man, as it passed out of this world. But I mean not now justice, in contrast to any overt profanation of it, out of greed, rare as such strict justice is. I mean intellectual injustice, such as we all perhaps have been guilty of, such as is with the utmost difficulty or perhaps never avoided, if men judge at all, wrong estimates of persons, actions, motives, characters, histories, feelings. That frequent appeal to the judgment of posterity in reversal of the unjust judgment of to-day; the almost proverbial saying, "Virtue in its good estate we envious hate; when withdrawn from our eyes we long for," attest the bias which we ourselves own that passion gives to our judgment. Yet the judgments are often rescinded as unreasonably as they were made. The world has ever on its lips the words "theological prejudice," meaning that *our* understandings are obscured by convictions which we hold indisputable, that *we* are blinded to the modern lights which would otherwise flash in upon us. But therewith it admits against itself the liability of the human intellect to be warped or blinded to the true Light through prejudice or preconceived opinion or whatever bias. Yet if, in the never-forgotten instance of Galileo, men trusted their senses or misinterpreted passages of Holy Scripture against conclusions of science which they did not understand, if believers have been wrongly suspicious of the interpreters of science, of which they knew but little, it is but part of our common human infirmity, that some schools of scientific research may be wrongly suspicious of interpreters of Scripture, and seem to prefer to find disharmony rather than harmony between the works and words of Almighty God, which may alike be misinterpreted but which cannot disagree.

But more widely—I speak throughout of tendencies of our nature, not, God forbid, of individuals—is it not violation of justice to employ different "weights and measures" in the things of nature and of God; in things of God to demand not evidence but demonstration, in theories upon the origin of man or of species, to assume that the possible is the real? or again, to question our so-attested Scriptures, and yet to appeal "to the lost leaves of the great book of nature" as establishing facts, which it is assumed that they *may* have contained; to deny the common origin of the different races of man, notwithstanding their essential oneness in power of communicating thought by speech or by writing, or of conceiving and worshipping God, and to affirm our common origin with certain of the brute creation incapable of either; to assume that miracles are impossible, because they are "contrary to experience," and yet to demand our assent to things in the long past, equally "contrary to experience;" to assume that in *their* case no "law of nature" was violated, since those changes, dissonant as they are from our experience, are referable to some higher, unknown law of physical development, and to deny that the Gospel-miracles are in conformity to some higher law of Divine Wisdom and Love, which lay in His Mind, " before the foundation of the world," and in view to which He regulated the laws of His physical creation; or, as in the Resurrection of our Lord, only forestall that which all we, who believe in a life to come, hope by His mercy will be fulfilled in ourselves; or again, to own that in every science, the unknown is more than the known, and to regard the mysteries of nature, as matters to be solved hereafter or to be left insoluble, but to regard mysteries in religion an irrefragable argument against it; in other words, to acknowledge that finite nature can contain what finite intelligence cannot explain, but since the finite cannot grasp the infinite, to disbelieve God because He is God, and to demand that God should lay aside His infinity, as a condition of our acknowledging, but not adoring Him; for how should the finite be the object of adoration?

What shall one say of want of love, that human passion, the mainspring of every thing noble or self-sacrificing in human nature, which the heathen scarce knew of as a virtue, but which, when engraced, soars on high to heaven from which it came, above all other virtues, even those sister graces, of which it alone shall abide when hope and faith pass away, the representative above all, and an effluence from God, for God is love? Love must needs be essential to the knowledge of God, for like only can understand like, and " God is love." " He that loveth not knoweth not God, for God is love." It is the living mirror of the Being of God, which is not mind alone or chiefly, but Love. But how is love, without which we cannot know God, contracted, distorted, warped, dulled, stupefied, extinguished, nay turned into hate by human evil passions! The mirror of the invisible God is clouded, darkened, troubled by every passion of our nature; so that it reflecteth not the hidden sun or stars or any fair form around, but only the dark cloud which lies heavy upon it and oppresses it. Selfishness disputes and abridges its realm, ambition dries it up, envy and jealousy empoison it; pride absorbs it and concentrates it around itself. Love heightens self-sacrifice, but without it self-sacrifice were but self-seeking: it is the soul of almsgiving; without it, profusion of gifts even to the poor were but an empty prodigality: it fired S. Paul's burning eloquence; without it, superhuman eloquence were but an empty profitless sound, superhuman knowledge an useless tinsel, miraculous power an unmeaning prodigy. Can its absence then, wherever it is absent, not be of mighty moment in hindering the clear sight of things divine? "With the heart," S. Paul says, "man believeth unto salvation [3]."

What can one say of the effect of that miserable counterfeit and antagonist of love, slavery to sensual passion? . "Whoredom and wine and new

---

[3] Rom. x. 10.

wine," says Hosea[4], "take away the heart." "Priest and prophet," says Isaiah[5] of his times, "have erred through strong drink, they are out of the way through strong drink; they err in vision, they stumble in judgment." Contrariwise our Lord says, "Blessed are the pure in heart: for they shall see God." But if it is the privilege of purity of heart to behold God for ever, how can they see Him in this vestibule and preparation for that eternal and beatific vision, who subject what is highest to what is lowest, the soul, which is most akin to God, to the passions of the flesh, which man has in common with the brutes? One need not say of it in common with all other sin, that they who habitually transgress God's laws must, like Felix, tremble at their awful sanction, "judgment to come," and wish that there were none. Indulgence of passion in itself dulls the mind to spiritual perceptions. "The natural (or animal) man receiveth not the things of the Spirit of God, for they are foolishness unto him, neither *can* he know them, because they are spiritually discerned[6]." The earthly mind becoming akin to the things which he dwells upon has no sense but for them; "to them he cleaves with the glue of love and wont; their image he carries back to his soul and converses with them, and, inured to them, is unable to think or imagine ought but what is

---

[4] Hosea iv. 11.   [5] Isa. xxviii. 7.   [6] 1 Cor. ii. 14.

corporeal[7]." He realizes not, of his own will, spiritual and divine things; for all is foolishness to him except what furnishes fuel to his passions, and, in the end, he *cannot* know them, because they are discerned by the God-enabled spirit of man, which he enslaves and immerses in the flesh, "Had they, whose intellect is now enslaved to evil," says Plato[8], "been in their youth severed from the leaden weights, with which they were born into the world, which hang on to sensual pleasure and drag them down and turn the vision of their souls about the things which are below—had they been released from these and turned round to the truth, the very same faculty," by which they see their way to their poor ends, "would have seen the other as keenly as they now see that on which their eye is fixed."

May you, my sons, never, by experience, know how sensual passion withdraws energy from intelligence, dulls the faculties, weakens the powers of reasoning, blunts the fineness of perception, indisposes to all spiritual things, induces, when habitual, scepticism as to the real duties of man, the reality of virtue, the sanctions of the laws of morality, or the freedom of the soul which it enslaves! Heathen mythology had a truth, which perhaps it knew not, when it represented its gods

[7] Taken from the author of the "De Vita Solitaria," quoted by à Lap. ad loc.
[8] Plato, Rep. l. c. ab. p. 10.

as transforming themselves into brute creatures when giving way to sensual passion.

Yet not active sin only, but mere inaction of faith blinds the intellect to the truths of God. "Faith without works is dead [9]," is a deep truth of our nature. Our faith lives in and by action; it was given us for action. The Gospel is not a philosophy, a speculation, an aggregate of opinions; it is a "power of God unto salvation[1]" putting itself forth in acts. Acts, enabled and brought into being by faith, nourish faith; they are essential to its health and well-being. Through acts of faith, God gives a conviction which is felt, more powerful than reasoning; discerning, above nature, Divine truth. Contrariwise inactive, unenergetic faith is a self-contradiction. Faith in truths above nature lawfully issues in acts above nature. Supernatural truth and supernatural life, i.e. a life of and from Divine Grace, belong together. A believer who acts not on his belief is a living lie. The world too owns this, when it urges the inconsistencies of a professed believer as an argument against belief. Their outward acts belie their inward convictions. If the acts correspond not to the faith, the faith will sink down to the acts. "Through this pride of rebellion against the light it cometh," says S. Gregory[2], "that because they will not do what they know, they come not to

[9] S. James ii. 26. [1] Rom. i. 16.
[2] S. Greg. l. xvi. in Job xxiv. 13, n. 70; Opp. i. 527, Ben.

know the good which they should do, but their own blindness shuts them out wholly from the light of truth." Since, then, by turns, the intellect becomes ultimately the slave of every passion and the heightener of every crime and sin, it is clearly no safeguard or bar against the charge of sin, that the immediate province of any act or series of acts lies in the intellect. Nor is its capacity of being warped limited to theology or morals, the special province of religion. It will slavishly dispute a truth wholly abstract, so soon as it perceives consequences, which it dislikes, which can be drawn from it. "Is number finite or infinite?" asked an eminent mathematician of others, the acutest minds in the university of France. If taken unawares, they answered "finite." "Then the universe had a beginning," was the necessary inference. Then forthwith those acutest intellects faltered, and sought to throw doubt on what they had just acknowledged as evident truth.

I have been speaking only of natural hindrances to the reception of Divine truth, faults, which, if unchecked, hinder the mind from seeing it, or turn away the soul from it. Hitherto, we have been on human ground. But there is one central underlying truth, that indulged sins or sinful tempers are opposed to and, in the end, repel the grace of God, through which alone man receives Divine faith. "No man cometh unto Me," our Lord saith, "unless My Father which hath sent Me draw him³." "It is written, They shall be all taught by God⁴." "No one knoweth the Son but the Father: neither knoweth any man the Father save the Son, and he to whomsoever the Son may reveal Him⁵." "I thank Thee, O Father, Lord of heaven and earth, that Thou hast hid these things [the truths of the Gospel] from the wise and prudent [in their own eyes] and hast revealed them unto babes⁶."

God forbid, that I should even seem to hint the thought, that the unbelief or misbelief of any individual was referable to any of these moral defects. God alone can judge the heart Who made it, and to Whom alone all its thoughts and intents are known. To his own master each will stand or fall. Enough for us to see, that moral defects are a hindrance to the reception of Divine truth; that those defects may be a means of forfeiting it; and that, whatever be the case of others, we are individually responsible, not only whether we have lived according to the light which God has given to each, but whether we, by not walking in the light, allowed darkness to come over us. They were very mainly spiritual faults, love of pre-eminence⁷, of tokens of reverence for their learning⁸, their devotion⁹, their preciseness of duty, of exactness in

---

³ S. John vi. 44.   ⁴ Ib. vi. 45.
⁵ S. Matt. xi. 27.   ⁶ Ib. xi. 25.
⁷ S. Matt. xxiii. 6, 7. S. Mark xii. 38, 39. S. Luke xi. 43; xx. 46.
⁸ S. Matt. xxiii. 7.   ⁹ Ib. 14.

keeping or guarding the law; their fair show of observance of things which yet, our Lord says, they "ought to have done[1]," which even misled those to whom our Lord first came, of whom chiefly S. John so sorrowfully says, "He came unto His own, and His own received Him not[2]." And so the more they saw, the more they were blinded. Through envy perhaps, that *His* coming, Who was to be their glory, was first made known to Gentiles, they directed the wise men where to find Him, themselves sought Him not. The more He revealed Himself, the more they hated Him. The more miracles He wrought, the more they set themselves against Him. They sifted His miracles; they could not deny the facts; and they sought the more to kill Him. The belief of the people embittered their unbelief. The miracle which, Spinoza said, he would believe if he saw it, decided them as to His death. "What do we? For this man doeth many miracles. If we let Him thus alone, all men will believe on Him[3]." "Perceive ye how ye prevail nothing? behold, the world is gone after Him[4]." When in the end, at the adjuration of Pilate, He declared who He was, in the words of Daniel's prophecy which they owned, they adjudged Him to death.

So verified they our Lord's words, "If ye were blind, ye should have no sin; but now ye say, We

[1] S. Matt. xxiii. 23.
[2] S. John i. 11.
[3] S. John xi. 47, 48.
[4] Ib. xii. 19.

see" [they convicted themselves that they did see]; "therefore your sin remaineth[5]." "If I had not come and spoken unto them, they had not had sin; but now they have no cloak for their sins[6]." "If I had not done among them the works which none other man did, they had not had sin; but now have they both seen and hated both Me and My Father[7]."

Every revelation of God, every interposition of His Providence, every added light, every motion of His grace, must needs involve a sifting time. The more the light shines, the more, through that free-will, with which God has endowed us, must men come into the light or retreat into darkness. The choice brings out what they were, and, if evil, aggravates it. "This is the condemnation, that light is come into the world, and men loved darkness rather than light, because their deeds were evil[8]." Intellectually they chose, passionately they loved darkness. The awful commission to Isaiah, and in him to all who declare the mind of God, "Say unto this people, Hear ye on and understand not; see ye on and know not. Make the heart of this people fat, and their ears heavy, and shut their eyes; lest they see with their eyes, and hear with their ears, and their heart understand and convert and be healed[9]," is fulfilled by man's free-will. The heart which will not receive God's

[5] S. John ix. 41.   [6] Ib. xv. 22.   [7] Ib. xv. 24.
[8] Ib. iii. 19.   [9] Isa. vi. 9, 10.

truth, becomes the more hardened against it the more it hears it.

"I am come," our Lord says, "a light into the world, that whosoever believeth on Me should not abide in darkness[1]." He came as the visible Revealer of the Father. Never, until by God's mercy we behold the Beatific Vision, and see God as He is, the Ever-blessed Three in One, did man or could man so closely behold God. "He that hath seen Me," our Lord says, "hath seen the Father[2]." For he saw *Him*, Who, under that human form which out of love for us He took, was Almighty God. His Godhead they could not see, but He Whom they saw was also, at that moment, "in the bosom of the Father[3], was "in Heaven[4]." They saw that Manhood, which had no separate existence, no Being, apart from Almighty God; Who, though He was God and Man, was not two, but one Christ; Whose Personality was not human but Divine. They saw Him Who shall be the joy of the blessed, Who shall, even when we see God, be, with God, the Light[5] of the Heavenly City. His words were the words of God. His eyes, whose look of Divine love won the Magdalen, so laden with sins, and Peter, after his awful fall, and the robber by His side on the Cross, must have shone with a Divine lustre on those who heard Him. His words

[1] S. John xii. 46. [2] Ib. xiv. 9.
[3] Ib. i. 18. [4] Ib. iii. 13.
[5] Rev. xxi. 23.

drew those, whom inwardly the Father drew[6], and at one word they left all and followed Him. And was there then no responsibility in leaving Him? Could so close a nearness to God not bring responsibility to those who rejected Him? Could it be without guilt, when men distorted those words, charged Him with confederacy with the Evil one, with blasphemy against His Father, Whose words He spake? Our Lord said, that there *would be* a judgment, though not *then*. *Then* was still the time of mercy; *then* there was still room for repentance; *then* the words spoken against the Son of Man could still be forgiven; nay our Lord enlarges to the utmost bound the contumelies against Himself which man in ignorance spake, which could yet be forgiven: "All manner of sin and blasphemy shall be forgiven unto men[7]," all, of which men should repent. But if any should finally reject Him, a judgment, beyond this world, still remained. "He that rejecteth Me, and receiveth not My words, hath one that judgeth him; the word that I have spoken, the same shall judge him in the last day." "He that rejecteth Me." Rejecteth Whom? Him, their God; Him, very God, Who "for us and our salvation became man;" Him, Who in the One Love of the Father and the Son, came into the world to save the world. "For God so loved the world that He gave His only-begotten Son, that whoso-

---

[6] S. John vi. 44. [7] S. Matt. xii. 31.

ever believeth in Him should not perish, but have everlasting life [8]."

It was not, then, only the rejection of a message or revelation of God, as though man had still been in a state of innocence, and God were unfolding fresh measures of knowledge of Himself, such as the Infinite God has in store for His saints in all eternity. This had been great insolence to God, could we conceive our first parents to have been guilty of it. It would seem a more hopeless fall than that which brought sin and death upon us, as being a more direct rejection of God. But now men have so come to be (as they think) on easy or equal terms with God, that, having ceased to think of Him as their Creator, they lose out of sight that they are not only His creatures, but guilty, rebel creatures; that God sent His Son into the world, not only or chiefly with a revelation of new truth to them, but of truth, by receiving which they might be saved. They forget that, by the manifold habitual breaking of God's laws, by offences, which they must themselves condemn and did condemn, they are sinners, wholly unfit to enter into His Presence, where " nothing defiled can enter [9];" incapable, through their manifold indulged and engrained evil passions, to find bliss in the presence of the All-holy, All-pure, All-loving God. The rejection then of Jesus was the rejection of the way devised by the love of God for their salvation.

[8] S. John iii. 16.   [9] Rev. xxi. 27.

Our race was, for our sins, under God's condemnation: we had set ourselves against Him; we had chosen evil against His good; we had misused His creatures against Himself; we had become a blot in the beauty of His creation; we had rebelled against Him, rejected Him as our Lord, become aliens from Him, disordered our nature, corrupted ourselves, defiled our souls, incapacitated ourselves for any participation in His Holiness or the bliss which He had prepared for them who love Him, to which in all eternity He destined each of us, if, on His terms, we would have Him. From first to last the object and end of the Gospel is, that man should be saved from his sins, by belief in Jesus. "His Name," it was said of Him before His birth, "shall be called Jesus: for He shall save His people from their sins [1]." This He declared to be His mission; this the prophets spake with one mouth; "To Him give all the prophets witness, that through His Name whosoever believeth in Him shall receive remission of sins [2]." "The Son of Man is come to seek and to save that which was lost [3]." This was the object of His coming into the world, "to save sinners [4]." "One Mediator there is between God and man, the Man Christ Jesus, Who gave Himself a ransom for all [5]." "Neither is there salvation in any other: for there

---

[1] S. Matt. i. 21. [2] Acts x. 43.
[3] S. Matt. xviii. 11. S. Luke xix. 10.
[4] 1 Tim. i. 15. [5] 1 Tim. ii. 5, 6.

is none other name under heaven given among men, whereby we must be saved [6]." It was then no new judgment, though all rejection of light must aggravate condemnation. They *were* already under condemnation; they refused Him through Whom God willed them to be saved; they *remained* under condemnation. So our Lord continues, "God sent not His Son into the world to condemn the world, but that the world through Him might be saved: he that believeth on Him is not condemned; but he that believeth not is condemned already, because he hath not believed in the name of the only-begotten Son of God [7]." And this was of their own will, whence our Lord says so mournfully, expostulatingly, to those who rejected and blasphemed Him, "Ye *will* not come unto Me, that ye might have life [8]." "I will it," He says, "but ye will it not;" as He says to Jerusalem, the slayer of the prophets, the stoner of those sent unto it, and soon to be His own crucifier: "How often did *I will* [9] to gather thee [1]" so tenderly under My fostering care, "and *ye willed not* [2]." Oh that mournful terrible power of the human will, which Almighty love wills to win, but which wills not to be won!

This, then, is the ground of that solemn sanc-

[6] Acts iv. 12.   [7] S. John iii. 17, 18.
[8] S. John v. 40.   [9] ἠθέλησα.
[1] S. Luke xiii. 34.   S. Matt. xxiii. 37.
[2] οὐκ ἠθελήσατε.

tion, with which our Lord accompanies His commission to His Apostles to teach all nations: "Go ye into all the world and preach the Gospel to every creature. He that believeth and is baptized shall be saved; he that believeth not shall be condemned [3]."

By the very force of the words, no one is included of all those generations who lived before Christ came, or whom the Gospel has not individually reached. The soul of the Church includes, we cannot doubt, "a great multitude whom no man could number, of all nations, and kindreds, and peoples, and tongues," who did not on earth belong to its body; as contrariwise believers, who led to the end bad lives and died impenitent, belonged, it may be, visibly to its body, but not to its soul. Jesus "died for all [4]." He was "a propitiation for the sins of the whole world [5];" for all, who have been since Adam's sin unto the end; for all, who have been or are or shall be; for all who knew Him or shall know Him, or who shall blamelessly know Him not; for those, who blindly "felt after [6]" Him or for some one or something to stand between them and their sins; who, by their hereditary although ignorant use of sacrifices, still acknowledged their guilt and separation from God; for those who, throughout the world, looked

---

[3] S. Mark xvi. 15, 16.   [4] 2 Cor. v. 14.
[5] 1 S. John ii. 2.   [6] Acts xvii. 27.

for a Deliverer to come; for those, who, by those "unutterable groanings," the mute restless longing of the human race, looked to the common Father of mankind. "We are taught," says St. Justin [7], "that Christ is the first-born of God, and we have shown above, that He is the Word, of whom the whole human race are partakers, and those who lived according to reason are Christians, even though accounted Atheists—so also they who have been before Him, and lived without reason, were worthless and enemies of Christ, and murderers of those who governed their lives by reason; but they who lived and live in accordance with reason are Christians, and are fearless and tranquil." But as to these indeed we need not witness from man. God has ruled it for us by S. Paul. "When the Gentiles which have not the law do by nature the things contained in the law, these, having not the law, are a law unto themselves, which show the work of the law written in their heart [8]." By whom could it be written, but by the Spirit of God?

But what of those, to whom the Gospel was preached and yet they did not receive it? To ask the question seems to answer it. If any one thinks of the variety of human minds, their inworked prejudices, the power of transmitted error, the startling novelty, to a Greek philosopher, of the

[7] Apol. i. n. 6, p. 35, Oxf. Tr.
[8] Rom. ii. 14.

Creation of the world, or the resurrection of the flesh, who would think, that our Lord's words, "He that believeth not shall be condemned," applied to all the philosophers on Mars' Hill, except the few who clave to S. Paul? Or, of the chosen people, who existed for the sake of Him Who was to be given through them, who would say that those words of our Lord applied to *all* the Jews at Rome who had only heard of Christianity as a "sect every where spoken against [9]"? Nay, since S. Paul speaks of his people as having "a zeal for God, though not according to knowledge [1]," who could venture even to think that the blindness which fell upon Israel was in all a guilty self-blinding? But if this was so when S. Paul was the preacher, how much more, if such as we cannot so present the truth to people's souls as to win them, must we not think that the fault may very probably be as much ours as theirs? Or, to take more distressing cases yet, who would say that the New Zealanders who, identifying the Christianity which they had received with the wrong dealings of Christians about their lands, went back to their idolatry; or those Indians in Mexico, who called Christianity the religion of their oppressors, and have gone wholly back to the idolatries which they held by a divided faith; or the Red Indians, whom Christian dealers decimated by what the Indian chief called our "fire-god," brandy, and who knew

[9] Acts xxviii. 22. [1] Rom. x. 2.

our Lord only as the God of those who had inflamed their passions and destroyed the health both of body and soul—who would say that, in these or any like cases, our Lord's words, "He that believeth not shall be condemned," would apply to all those, who, under such circumstances, hearkened not to His message or apostatised from the faith in Him? Nay more, the Church, while it repeats our Lord's warnings, would not, and has not ventured to pronounce upon the loss of any one individual soul of man, unless, as in the case of Judas, God Himself seems to have declared it. "We take good heed," says an accredited writer[2], "never to affirm positively the reprobation of any one in particular, whatever have been his religion, country, period, nay, his conduct. In the soul, at the last moment of its passage on the threshold of eternity, there occur doubtless Divine mysteries of justice, but above all, of mercy and of love; 'mercy triumpheth over justice.' We abstain from sounding indiscreetly the Divine counsels, but we know indubitably that on each occasion they are worthy of God and of His infinite goodness as well as of His justice."

Our Lord's words, then, announce a principle of God's judgment; they tell us where and how we are in safety; who, if to the end they continue to reject Him, must be rejected by Him. As to faith, equally with God's moral law, God tells us what incapacitates us for His presence in bliss.

[2] P. Ravignan, Confér. 36, t. ii. p. 521.

But in both alike we are forbidden, under sanctions as awful, to usurp as to individuals *His* prerogative, Who is our common Judge. We dare not, as the Heathen did, imagine in hell those stained with crimes, of guilt undeniable [3]. " Judge not," our Lord commands us, "judge not, that ye be not judged [4]." " Judge nothing before the time, until the Lord come, Who both will bring to light the hidden things of darkness and make manifest the counsels of the hearts [5]."

And if it be so as to those who did not receive the personal faith in Jesus, whom His Divine tenderness could not melt, His Divine love could not win, His Divine holiness could not awe, to whom He stretched out in vain those sacred Hands for them pierced, to whom He cried in vain, " Come unto Me and I will receive you, I will cleanse you from your sins, and give you victory and life and love ;" if even those who wholly disbelieved in Him, nay, it must be said disbelieved Him, may yet be saved by Him, how much less does the Church pronounce that any individual is lost, who, however imperfectly, believes in Him, though it may be, like the Samaritan woman, they know not who He is. He has said, " Whoso cometh unto Me, I will in no wise cast out," and the Church could not doubt that any one who,

---

[3] Virgil wrote of Theseus, &c., according to the popular belief, which he himself believed not. Dante names individuals, as instances of sins, through which souls are lost, but with no authority from the Church and against its rules.
[4] S. Matt. vii. 1.   [5] 1 Cor. iv. 5.

with an honest and true heart, sought Him would be found of Him, that He would rather appear to such a soul invisibly, as He did to Saul when breathing out threatenings and slaughter against His disciples and persecuting Himself in them, than that such a soul should perish. Such may misbelieve of Him. It is to their great loss that they know not Who He is Who loves them. According to their light, they still believe Him.

The Church would not pronounce even upon the authors of heresy, widely-desolating as their errors have been. To their own Master they have stood or fallen. But it is acknowledged, that hereditary misbelief mitigates the responsibility of individuals. Heresy loses some of its virus by transmission. Voluntary and culpable rejection of God's truth, bad faith, perversity of will, alone, condemn. Hereditary Nestorians or Eutychians, although they deny the Incarnation; hereditary Anti-Trinitarians or Mohammedans, although they believe in God as other than He is, are not responsible, unless the light comes to them from within or from without, and they, of their own will, shut their eyes, and will not look at it, or turn away from or reject it, and God in it. "They," said the great teacher of our Western Christendom who during his whole converted life toiled in winning back to the faith those who had erred from it, Manichees, Arians, Donatists, Pelagians, Priscillianists, "They who without any pertinacious contentiousness defend their sentiment, however false and perverse, especially such as they did not themselves originate by the rashness of their own presumption, but have received it from parents who were misled and fell into error, and who seek the truth with careful solicitude, ready to be amended when they find it, these are no wise to be accounted heretics [6]." Obviously; since the very term " heretics " implies a perverse choice of will. " Let those," he says again to that strange sect who had deluded his early youth by promises of unmixed truth, " let those be fierce towards you, who know not with how great toil truth is found, how difficultly errors are avoided. Let those be fierce towards you, who know not how rare and arduous a thing it is to overcome carnal phantasms by the serenity of a pious mind, or they who know not with how great difficulty the eye of the inner man is healed, so that it can behold its sun—' the Sun of Righteousness,' the ' true Light' which lighteneth every man that cometh into the world.' Let those be fierce towards you, who know not, with what sighs and groans men attain, in any ever so small a degree, to understand God. Lastly, let those be fierce against you, who were never deceived by the like error whereby they see you deceived [7]."

No! That word of God stands sure, "In every

[6] Ep. 43. Glorio, &c., init.
[7] Ep. cont. Manich. c. 2, Opp. viii. 151, 152.

nation he that feareth God and worketh righteousness is accepted with Him [8]." For the Lover and Father of mankind, Who willeth not that any should perish, has not one way only of bringing home His lost sheep. All who shall be saved, shall be saved for the sake of that Precious Blood, which has redeemed our earth and arrayed it with Divine glory and beauty. Varied and beautiful, each with its special loveliness, will be the choirs of His elect. In those ever-open portals there enter, day and night, that countless multitude of every people, nation, and language; they who, in the Church, were by His grace faithful to Him, and they who knew not the Church of God, whom the Church below knew not how to win, or alas! neglected to win them, but whom Jesus looked upon, and the Father drew to Himself, whom His inner light enlightened, and who, out of the misery of our fallen state, drawn by His unknown grace, looked up yearningly to Him, their "unknown God," yet still *their* God, for He made them for Himself. There, out of every religion or irreligion, out of every clime, in whatever ignorance steeped, in whatever hatred or contempt or blasphemy of Christ nurtured, God has His own elect, who ignorantly worship Him, whose ignorant fear or longing He Who inspired it will accept.

No! ask any tolerably-instructed Christian

[8] Acts x. 35.

person, and his instinct will respond what every teacher of the Church every where knows to be truth. Ask him, "Will any soul be lost, heathen, idolater, heretic, or in any form of hereditary unbelief or misbelief, if in good faith he was what he was, living up to the light which he had, whencesoever it came, and repenting him where he did amiss?" All Christendom would answer you, God forbid! He would not be "'saved by that law which he professeth [9]," but he would be saved *in* it, by the one love of God the Father Who made him, and of God the Son Who redeemed him, and God the Holy Ghost Who drew, and in his measure sanctified him.

It has been through a strange ignorance, I may almost say, of Christianity itself, which at all times has condemned the error of those who denied the Lord Who brought them, but has never pronounced on individuals, that this sudden storm has been raised against,

> "The Psalm that gathers in one glorious lay,
> All chants that e'er from heaven to earth found way:
> Creed of the Saints, and Anthem of the Blest,
> And calm-breathed warning of the kindliest love
> That ever heaved a wakeful mother's breast[1]:"

as though it condemned to the eternal loss of God, —at one time people said, the whole Greek Church, though that Church would not except against the

---

[9] Article xviii.
[1] Lyra Apostolica, cxv. Athanasian Creed. John Keble.

truth of its formula, rightly explained; at another, two eminent Divines of our own, defenders of the faith, who contradict, of course, no truth therein; at another, all those who without any fault of their own are ignorant of or contradict the truth.

Strange perversion of the first principle of the judgment of the Church, which while, following its Lord, it condemns denials of the faith, with Him leaves all individuals to the judgment of the great day; " that word shall judge him at the last day," on which no one will be condemned who acted in good faith, who did not, face to face, reject his God. "The Church," it has been well said, "has its long list of saints; it has not inserted *one* name in any catalogue of the damned."

And against what is this sudden whirlwind raised? Against the simplest confession which could be made of the Being of God and of our Lord Jesus Christ. Look well at it. There is not a single abstract term used; there is not one statement in it, in relation to the Holy Trinity or the Incarnation, which, if it were denied, God or our Lord Jesus Christ would remain the same Being. If any were to deny that the Father, the Son, and the Holy Ghost, were each Uncreate, Infinite, Eternal, Almighty, Lord, he would deny that they were God: if he were to assert that there were Three, Uncreated, Infinite, Eternal, Almighty, Lord, he would deny that God is One. They are but so many notes of one Divine harmony, prolonged, because the Church loved to dwell in adoring love upon the Being of its Author and its End, Almighty God; because it loved to dwell on and would impress on us the thought of the absolute perfection of each; how Each was wholly all which we can conceive of God, and yet that God is absolutely One. It does not raise questions; it rests the soul in the contemplation (as we can here) of the Co-eternal, Co-equal, Three, in their adorable Oneness.

Or again as to the Incarnation of our Lord Jesus Christ, that wonderful Creed explains to us difficulties of Holy Scripture, which remain difficulties to those who do not receive it, as, "My Father is greater than I[2]." Its words are a shield to our faith, and an instruction to it. Some of the heresies which it tacitly corrects are so natural to the mind, and yet it corrects them so uncontroversially, so devotionally; every word in it is an antidote against a heresy which would annihilate our faith, and yet we pass over them unheeded; they jar not upon us, and our faith sinks the more intelligently and deeper into our souls, while we have been praising the unutterable mercy of our God, who "for us men and for our salvation" "became Man." Here again are no abstract propositions, such as there must be about many of the Christian truths. Every word relates to the Person of our Lord. They, whose wrong teaching the Creed tacitly cor-

[2] S. John xiv. 28.

rects, taught in effect, that our Lord was not God, or was not Man, or that if once Man He has ceased to be Man. Not a single statement could be denied, and our Lord yet any longer be He Whom we love and adore, Very God, and for our sakes, Very Man.

And are not then our people to be warned, that if we deny Him Who came to save us, we incur the loss of our salvation? But then why did our Lord say, "He that believeth not is condemned already, because he hath not believed in the name of the Only-begotten Son of God [3]"? Why, to the Jews who asked, "What shall we do, that we might work the works of God?" did He answer, "This is the work of God, that ye believe [4] on Him, Whom He hath sent"? It cannot be thought that our Lord meant them to believe in Him, other than He was. Why is it said, "He that believeth not the Son shall not see life, but the wrath of God abideth on him [5]"? or, "If ye believe not that I am He, ye shall die in your sins [6]"? Or why did the Apostle of love, he whom Jesus loved, who lay in His Bosom, sum up his Gospel, "These things are written, that ye might believe that Jesus is the Christ, the Son of God; and that believing ye might have life in His Name [7]"? Why to the affrighted jailor, who asked, "What shall I do to be

[3] S. John iii. 18.   [4] Ib. vi. 28, 29.
[5] Ib. iii. 36.   [6] Ib. viii. 24.
[7] Ib. xx. 31.

saved?" did S. Paul say, "Believe on the Lord Jesus Christ, and thou shalt be saved, and thy house [8]"? Believe on Him, surely, as He is, not, as He is not. Or S. Peter, "Through His Name whosoever believeth in Him shall receive remission of sins [9]"? Or why did S. John warn, "Every spirit that confesseth not that Jesus Christ is come in the flesh is not of God; and this is that spirit of Antichrist whereof ye have heard that it should come [1]"? Or S. Peter, of "damnable heresies, even denying the Lord that bought them, and bring upon themselves quick destruction [2]"? People talk carelessly about "affirming that the salvation of the soul depends upon the assent of the intellect to this, that, or the other theological proposition." Theology, of course, has its province, in ordering the relation of revealed truths; but look well at the Athanasian Creed, and you will find nothing in regard to our Lord Jesus Christ, which is not essential to *His* Being, in Whom you hope to be saved.

This great Creed is clearer than the other Creeds; it explains to the simple, or the heathen convert, the first truths of the Christian faith. Missionary Bishops have felt its value. The African, in his untaught simplicity, thanks God for the glorious light which it sheds on what in the Nicene Creed was difficult to him. I should think that wellnigh every thoughtful believer must have felt how

[8] Acts xvi. 30, 31.
[9] Ib. x. 43.
[1] 1 S. John iv. 3.
[2] 2 S. Pet. ii. 1.

God, through it, had taught him to think aright upon subjects upon which he *must* think. And for those clauses, which press upon us our own responsibility as to truth which God has made known to us, that we cannot be as the Heathen who know it not, I suppose that, not until the Day of Judgment shall we know their inestimable value to us. True charity is to warn of the existence of a precipice; it were unloving to men's souls to leave them playing close to it, but unwarned.

> " Who knows but myriads owe their endless rest
> To thy recalling, tempted else to rove[3]?"

Let any one fix in his mind, how he would explain those words of the Gospel, upon which they are founded, and he will not be at a loss how they themselves are to be explained.

This tornado will, I trust by God's mercy, soon pass; it is a matter of life and death. To remove those words or the Creed because it contains them, would be emphatically to teach our people, that it is *not* necessary to salvation to believe faithfully the Incarnation of our Lord Jesus Christ, or in our God as He has made Himself known to us. It would be to be ashamed of Him and of His words, upon which those words are founded.

And for you, my sons, remember that all this which I have said about the non-responsibility of those, who in any way, through ignorance or preju-

[3] John Keble, l. c.

dice by them invincible, are hindered from receiving the truth, has a reverse side to you. We "are not of the darkness [4]." Us "God hath called out of darkness into His marvellous light [5]." To us *He* says Who is the true Light, "Walk while ye have the light, lest darkness come upon you; for he that walketh in darkness knoweth not whither he goeth. While ye have light, believe in the light, that ye may be the children of light [6]." God excuses unblamable, ignorance. He says by His Apostle, "the times of ignorance God winked at [7]." He has recovered those who through unfavourable circumstances of their surroundings, through the malformation of an almost natural scepticism, through doubt infused into them, perhaps through rash venturing in depths which they could not sound, or being, like him who became S. Augustine, seduced by those who promised him larger light, have lost their faith. God's mercies are boundless, or bounded only by our willingness to receive them. But of all hopeless cases, the most hopeless would seem unbelief engendered by levity. Yet such, I hear, still lingers among some of you, my sons. They speak of some who become " positivists " through whatever bias of their own; of others, who (to use a term of your own) " follow suit," throwing off their faith as they would a worn-out dress, because it is not fashionable with those, whose esti-

[4] 1 Thess. v. 5.
[5] 1 S. Pet. ii. 9.
[6] S. John xii. 35, 36.
[7] Acts xvii. 30.

mation of cleverness they esteem more than the good favour of Him Who is Infinite Wisdom. A prophet of heathenism and its highest intellect yet speaks to you, " My son, you are young, and the advance of time will make you renounce many of the opinions which you now hold. Wait therefore until the time comes, and do not attempt to judge of high matters at present; and that is the highest of which you think nothing—to know the gods rightly and to fear accordingly. Of one thing of great importance I am quite certain; you and your friends are not the first who have held this about the gods. There have always been persons more or less numerous, who have had the same disorder. I have known many of them, and can tell you this, that no one who had taken up in youth this opinion, that the gods do not exist, ever continued in the same till he was old. What may be the true doctrine, if you are patient, you will hereafter discover. Meantime take heed that you offend not about the gods [3]."

But you, if you despised or lightly set at nought God's revelation of Himself, would sin against light and love, which Plato knew not of. We have a responsibility, wholly different in kind from that which he had, or any one who, at this day, by circumstances of his birth, is outside of Christianity

---

[3] Plato de Legg. l. x. p. 888; vol. iv. p. 398, Jowett's Translation.

or of its full truth. In God's individual love for each of you, He has given you the faith, whereby you may be saved. You have not to learn it; you have only, not to unlearn it. No one scarcely loses his faith at once. It is so precious to the soul, that God does not, unless driven forth from the soul by things or tempers incompatible with His Presence, cease, even amid continued provocation, to continue that grace whereby alone we can retain it. But there are many preparations for that loss. At your age, the idle word, the repetition of the profane jest, the listening to, it may be, some pointed scoff at some un-understood character or phrase of Scripture, the first ashamedness of truth, because it is old, or, as some will tell you, antiquated, the first wish not to seem less advanced or enlightened than others, or less free from theological prejudice, or not to be behind the age (as it calls itself), or to be accounted as talented as any talented equal, who may, alas! have lost his faith :—these are the distant, and not always distant, preparations for the loss of faith. For they treat God with levity and prefer the creature to the Creator. "How can ye believe," our Lord said, " which receive honour one of another, and seek not the honour which cometh from God only [9]?" It is known that not long ago the young here often lost their faith, because they came ready to part

[9] S. John v. 44

with it. Then follow, careless reading of books against faith, or truth, or, it may be, the being of God, which have their answers, but which answers, it may be, your thought or knowledge may not be matured enough to interpose between the suggested doubts and your soul. Then follow, alas! or accompany it, some of those tempers, pride or vainglory or the like, which shut out God, because they set up an idol, self, in His temple, your souls. "Love truth," said an experienced writer [1], almost proverbial for gentleness and love; "love truth as much as you love your health, your vanity, your pleasure, your phantasy; you will find it." It is a sore thing in the end to part with God, Who made you, and redeemed you at such a price, that you might share His endless love. Draw nigh unto Him in truthfulness, and He Who secretly draws you will draw nigh to you; seek Him, and He Who willeth to be found, He who sought you, will be found of you; part not with Him wilfully and because you prefer, to Him something which is not He, and He will not depart from you.

> "Of penitents sole hope and stay,
> To wandering sinners kind;
> To those who seek Thou art the Way;
> But what to those who find!"

God grant, when the time of your departure shall be at hand, each of you may be able to say

---

[1] Fénélon, "Lettre sur les moyens donnés aux hommes pour arriver à la vraie Réligion." Œuvres, Classe i., t. i. p. 426.

with the aged Paul, in view of *his*, "I have fought the good fight; I have finished my course, I have kept the faith;" and "the Lord, the righteous Judge, give you in that day the crown of righteousness laid up, not for him only, but for all those who love His appearing [2]."

NOTE A, on p. 11.

Passages from S. Cyril of Alexandria, in which he speaks of the Holy Spirit as proceeding from the Son.

P. PÉTAU (de Trin. vii. 3. Opp. Theol. ii. 369) quotes the following passages of S. Cyril:—

1. "The Holy Spirit is the Spirit of God and the Father, and of the Son also, being poured forth essentially from Both, viz. from the Father through the Son" (τὸ οὐσιωδῶς ἐξ ἀμφοῖν —προχεόμενον). De Adorat. l. i. p. 9. Aub.

2. "For in that the Son is God, and of (ἐκ) God by nature (for He is truly Begotten of (ἐκ) God the Father), the Spirit is His very Own, and in Him and from Him (ἴδιον αὐτοῦ καὶ ἐν αὐτῷ τε καὶ ἐξ αὐτοῦ), just as it is conceived as to God the Father."

3. "He infused not into the baptized a Spirit foreign (to Himself) in manner of a servant and minister; but, as being by nature God, with supremest power, He sent the Spirit

---

[2] From 2 Tim. iv. 7, 8.

which was from Him and His very own" (τὸ ἐξ αὐτοῦ τε καὶ ἴδιον αὐτοῦ). De Recta Fide ad Theod. Imp. Opp. t. v. P. ii. p. 33.

4. "The Only-Begotten Word of God, when He became Man, remained then, too, God, being all which the Father is, save being the Father, and, having as His own, the Holy Spirit, which is *from* Him and essentially inexisting in Him" (τὸ ἐξ αὐτοῦ καὶ οὐσιωδῶς ἐμπεφυκὸς αὐτῷ Πνεῦμα ἅγιον). Explan. xii. capp. Expl. ix. Opp. vi. 154, 155.

5. In the Thesaurus, Ass. 34, "That the Spirit is God and hath the same operation with the Son, and is not alien from His Essence, and that, when God is said to dwell in us, it is the Holy Spirit who indwelleth," he has a heading, "That the Holy Spirit is of the Essence of the Father and the Son;" and says, "Since the Holy Spirit, coming to be in us, makes us conformed to God, and He goeth forth from the Father and the Son, He is manifestly of the Divine Essence, being essentially in It, and going forth from It; as, in a way, that breath which goeth forth from the mouth of man; poor and inadequate as the instance is, for God is above all" (Opp. vi. 345).

6. "Since Christ giveth laws, the Spirit, as being by nature in Him and from Him (ἐν αὐτῷ καὶ ἐξ αὐτοῦ φυσικῶς ὑπάρχον) Himself giveth laws" (Ib. p. 354).

7. "Since, when Christ reneweth us, and removeth us into a new life, the Spirit reneweth us, we must of necessity confess that the Spirit is of the Essence of the Son. For, as being by nature of Him (ἐξ αὐτοῦ κατὰ φύσιν ὑπάρχον), and being sent by Him upon the creation, He worketh the renovation, being the Complement of the Holy Trinity. But if so, the Spirit is God and of God, and not a creature" (Ib. p. 358). Where, as P. Pétau observes, S. Cyril proves that He is of God (ἐκ θεοῦ) because *He is by nature of* the Son. It cannot then refer to any temporal Procession.

8. Some arguers inferred that "when the Son said of Himself and of the Spirit, that 'He shall take of Mine and shall show it unto you,' He indicated a difference of nature," S. Cyril

answers, "Not at all. For how should that Spirit, which is both from Him and in Him and His very own (τὸ ἐξ αὐτοῦ τε καὶ ἐν αὐτῷ καὶ ἴδιον αὐτοῦ), partake of Him, and be sanctified relatively like those things which are without, and be by nature alien from *Him*, Whose very Own He is said to be?" De S. Trin. l. vii. Ib. p. 657.

9. "How shall we separate the Spirit from the Son, thus inexisting and being essentially united, Who cometh forth through Him, and is by nature in Him? The blessed Paul, having named 'the Spirit of Christ dwelling in us,' forthwith subjoined, ' If Christ is in you,' introducing an entire likeness of the Son with the Spirit, Who is His very Own and is by nature poured forth from Him" (τὸ ἴδιον αὐτοῦ καὶ παρ' αὐτοῦ κατὰ φύσιν προχεόμενον Πνεῦμα). In S. John i. 33, pp. 126, 127.

10. "For although the Spirit is in His own Person, and is conceived of by Himself, in that He is Spirit and not Son, yet is He not alien from Him; for He is named the Spirit of truth, and Christ is the Truth, and He is poured forth from Him, just as He is from God the Father" (Ep. ad Nest. Opp. v. P. ii. p. 74).

11. "He sent to us the Comforter from heaven, through Whom and in Whom He is in us, and dwelleth in us, not infusing into us an alien, but the own Spirit of His Essence and of that of His Father" (τὸ τῆς οὐσίας αὐτοῦ καὶ τῆς τοῦ Πατρὸς αὐτοῦ ἴδιον Πνεῦμα). De Trin. Dial. 7, p. 642.

12. "Since He is the Spirit of Christ and His Mind, He knoweth what is in Him—wherefore, as knowing all things which are in the counsel of the Only-Begotten, He reporteth all things to us, not having that knowledge from learning, that He may not seem to fulfil the rank of a minister, and to transmit the words of another, but as His Spirit, and knowing untaught all of Him, from Whom and in Whom He is (ἐξ οὗ καὶ ἐν ᾧπέρ ἐστί), He revealeth to the holy the Divine mysteries. In a manner as the human mind, knowing all which is in it, ministereth externally by uttered word, the

wills of the soul, whereof it is the mind, being mentally discerned in the thoughts, and named as something else than itself, but being by nature no other, but as a part, complemental of the whole, both being it and being believed to go forth from it." In S. Joann. l. 10, p. 837.

13. My son suggests, as like to these, the last words of his tenth book on S. John (p. 926): "For this cause He added, 'He shall show you the things to come,' all but saying, 'This shall be a sign unto you that the Spirit is altogether *from* My substance (ἐκ τῆς ἐμῆς οὐσίας), and is, as it were, My Mind, that He shall show you the things to come, even as I. For this He could not have done, without being altogether in Me, and going forth through Me, and being of the same substance with Me."

14. And from the Commentary on S. Luke, translated by the Very Rev. Dr. P. Smith, from a Syriac Version: " Nor has He [the Divine Word, become Man] need of the Holy Ghost: for the Spirit that proceedeth from the Father is of Him and equal to Him in substance" (P. i. p. 46).

As a guarantee against the ordinary Greek imputation of falsification of the texts by Latinizers, my son, the present editor of S. Cyril, tells me that, of these passages, No. 3 is extant in a contemporary translation by Rabbula, Bp. of Edessa; No. 4 is in an *old* Syriac translation; Nos. 5, 6, 7, he found in a MS. in the Patriarchal Library at Cairo; No. 1 is in a Bodleian MS. which was given to its possessor by a Greek Patriarch about the end of the fifteenth century; No. 14 is extant only in the Syriac.

But, over and above the force of single passages, is their multiplicity, showing that this was the habitual thought and faith of that great Father. In the Commentary on S. John alone, my son's Index refers to nine passages in which S. Cyril says, that " all things are through the Son in the Holy Spirit;" twenty-five in which he calls Him " the own Spirit of the Son;" seven, in which he names Him, " the Spirit of the Father and the Son ;" one, in which "the own Spirit of the Father and the Son ;" and twice, "the own Spirit, as of the Father so of the Son ;" once, "inseparable from the Son ;" thrice, "proceedeth from the Father by the Son ;" twice, "is of the Essence of the Son ;" he calls Him also in different places, "the Countenance" ($\pi\rho\acute{o}\sigma\omega\pi o\nu$), "the Image," "the Likeness" of the Son; five times he says, "is in the Son and goeth forth from the Son ;" once, that "the Spirit goeth forth from the Substance of the Only-Begotten, being nothing else than He, as to identity of substance, save that He exists in His own Person" (l. xi. p. 925); seven times, that "He is the Spirit of Truth because He is the Spirit of Christ, Who is the Truth."

I have accumulated these passages, because I have observed here and there, a disposition to abandon the "Filioque" in the Nicene Creed also, in the vain hope of conciliating the Greeks. Among *us*, who have not the ancient tradition of the Greeks, that "the Holy Spirit proceedeth from the Father through ($\delta\iota\grave{\alpha}$) the Son" (which the Council of Florence acknowledged to have the same meaning as our Western formula), the abandonment of the "Filioque" would speedily issue in heresy, believing and thinking of God, as other than He Is. See further, the Rev. G. Williams's Article on "The Orthodox Greek Church" in "The Church and the Age," Second Series, pp. 231 sqq.

APPENDIX.

Reply to Bishop Moberly's Argument against the Warning Clauses of the Athanasian Creed.

BISHOP MOBERLY'S argument against the warning clauses of the Athanasian Creed is founded upon a misconception both of those clauses and of the Creed itself, as strange as it is sad and unlooked for. In these days of severance, old age itself has no exemption from these severances between those who hoped they had fought the good fight together as friends.

This argument involves the following arbitrary assumptions: —1. That what the Apostles taught as matters of faith in obedience to our Lord's commission, "Go ye into all the world, and preach the Gospel to every creature," is limited to what is, in the letter, contained in their recorded sermons in the Acts. 2. That consequently our Lord's warning words, "He that believeth not shall be condemned," apply only to the teaching so recorded. 3. That all other matters of faith, embodied by the Church in her Creeds, lie in the word "baptized," and that our Lord purposely omitted that word in the second clause, "He that believeth not shall be condemned," in order to intimate that the penalty of loss of salvation may be affirmed only of those points of faith which Bishop Moberly has selected as belonging to the word "believe," not of those which he has relegated to the word "baptized," these being, he thinks, mingled with human infirmity. 4. That those words of our

Lord must be understood with some restrictions as to individuals, God alone being the Judge, what want of distinct faith entails this penalty upon any one, what does not; but that the same reference to the judgment of God as to individuals is not to be allowed in regard to the sentences of the Athanasian Creed, which are founded on these words of our Lord.

i. The faith which Bishop Moberly supposes the Apostles to have alone preached, and alone to have been contained in our Lord's words, "preach the Gospel to every creature," and so alone to come under our Lord's awful sanction, he derives from S. Peter's sermon to Cornelius [1], and sums up in the following terms [2]:—

"It is the preaching of the great Gospel facts, the Incarnation and Birth of the Son of God, of His holy life and example, of His Atoning Death upon the Cross, of His Resurrection from the dead, of His Ascension into Heaven, of the descent of the Holy Ghost to dwell in the Church, of the certainty of the future judgment of quick and dead."

I should have thought it more scriptural to say, that it was to "believe in our Lord Jesus," which involves the believing in Him, as He is, God and Man, and in what He has revealed.

The assumption that the Apostles' preaching in the Acts represents the whole of the teaching of the Apostles, by virtue of our Lord's commission, and so alone comes under the sanction of His awful words, certainly does not commend itself, even at first sight, I should think, to any simple mind.

a. The preaching, recorded in the Acts, is almost always the *first* addressed to the persons there assembled, and so is very elementary. In the one exception to this, viz. the exhortation to "the elders of the Church" at Ephesus [3], we have the remarkable expression, "The Church of God [4], which He hath purchased with His own Blood."

---

[1] Acts x. 36—43.   [2] Sermon, p. 45.   [3] Acts xx. 18—35.
[4] Dean Alford, also, after the discovery of the Sinaitic MS., acknowledged this as the right reading.

b. Converts were, by our Lord's command, "baptized [5] into the name of the Father and of the Son and of the Holy Ghost." This is implied also in the Acts, since, when some disciples at Ephesus answered that they did not know of the being of the Holy Ghost, S. Paul asked, "Unto what then were ye baptized [6] ?" Had they known Christian Baptism, they must have heard of Him, since it is Baptism "into the Name of" the Holy Trinity, "Father, Son, and Holy Ghost." All those who were baptized must have known the doctrine of the Holy Trinity. Baptism was the embodying of our Creed, a living Creed, and the safeguard against every heresy as to the All-holy Trinity in Whom we believe, into Whose Name we are baptized. "Jesus," S. Chrysostome says [7], "commandeth the Apostles to pour themselves over the whole world, giving into their hands a summary of their teaching, that, namely, through Baptism." "To those who believe," says S. Hilary [8], "that word of God were sufficient, which was poured into our ears by the testimony of the Evangelist together with the very power of His truth [viz. in baptism] when the Lord saith, 'Go now and teach all nations, baptizing them in the Name of the Father and of the Son and of the Holy Ghost, &c.' For what of the mystery of man's salvation is not contained therein? Or what is omitted or left obscure? All things are full, as from Him who is Fulness, and perfect, as from Perfection.'" "For neither," argues S. Athanasius [9], "did He conjoin an angel with the Godhead, nor did He unite us with Himself and the Father in one created, but in the Holy Spirit." "Leave off," saith yet another [1], "your controversy with men, and resist, if thou canst, the words of the Lord, which laid down for men the invocation in Baptism."

---

[5] St. Matt. xxviii. 19.   [6] Acts xix. 2, 3.   [7] Ad loc.
[8] De Trin. l. ii. init.
[9] Ep. 1 ad Serap. c. 11, p. 660.
[1] S. Greg. Nyss. in Bapt. Christi, p. 372. See more fully in the writer's "Scriptural Doctrine of Holy Baptism," pp. 68—80.

Whence alike Eusebius [2], while suppressing for the time the word "of one substance," and S. Hilary declaring, that when the Creed, as settled at Nicæa, had not reached to Gaul [3], he understood the "of one substance," declare that they received the faith in the Holy Trinity at their Baptism. "Thus," S. Hilary says to God [4], "I believed in Thee; by Thee I was thus reborn; and thenceforth I am Thine."

c. There seems no doubt, from the text of the Acts itself, that S. Peter taught that repentance is the gift of God [5] (which contradicts in principle the Pelagian heresy), and that S. Paul taught the resurrection of the body in his disputations at Athens; for the mockery which he met with, attached, in the minds of the heathen, not to the immortality of the soul, but to the resurrection of the flesh, which indeed alone is "resurrection." And this is spoken of as a Gospel—"he preached unto them the good tidings of Jesus and the resurrection [6]"—($τὴν ἀνάστασιν εὐηγγελίζετο$). He must also have taught that Jesus is an Object of worship, since they spoke of him as "a setter forth of strange gods;" and [although not as contained in that public teaching] he taught the necessity of "continuing in the *grace of God* [7]," and from his first conversion inculcated on Jew and Gentile, that they should "do works meet for repentance [8]." Our Lord also, in the commission which He gave him, directed him to speak of "the inheritance among them which are *sanctified* by faith which is in Me [9];" words which re-appear in his farewell sermon to the elders of Ephesus [10], but nowhere else in the Acts; so elementary was that recorded teaching.

d. S. Paul is recorded sometimes to have spent long periods at the same place. He and Barnabas "spent a whole year at"

---

[2] "As we have received from the Bishops, who preceded us, and in our first catechisings, and when we received the holy laver—so believing also at the time present, we report our faith."—S. Ath. Nic. Def. App. 2, pp. 59, 60, Oxf. Tr.

[3] De Synod. p. 1205. [4] De Trin. vi. 21. [5] Acts v. 31
[6] Ib. xvii. 18. [7] Ib. xiii. 43. [8] Ib. xxvi. 20.
[9] Ib. xxvi. 18. [10] Ib. xx. 32.

Appendix. 65

Antioch[11]; some years afterwards we hear of his "continuing[1]" there "teaching and preaching the word of the Lord:" at Corinth he abode "for a year and six months teaching the word of God among them[2]," and for "yet a good while[3]", after he had been brought before Gallio: at Ephesus he spent a period of "three years[4]," in which for three months[5] he disputed "in the synagogues, and persuaded the things concerning the kingdom of God," or having "separated the disciples," still "disputed daily in the school of Tyrannus," yet all the while, exercising the pastoral office, "warning every one night and day with tears, declaring unto them the whole counsel of God," and that in part with the view of guarding them against heretical teachers, who, he says, "I know, will enter in after my departure[6]." At Rome also he "dwelt two whole years[7] in his own hired house, and received all that came in unto him, preaching the kingdom of God, and teaching those things which concern the Lord Jesus Christ." Now it is quite impossible to conceive that in all these long series of preaching and teaching, S. Paul should have confined himself to those elementary truths of the Gospel which the Apostles dwelt upon in their first preachings to the unconverted. And accordingly,

e. The Epistles presuppose that they to whom they were written, were already in possession of a large body of teaching beyond those first elements which Bishop Moberly has extracted from S. Peter's sermon. S. Paul directly asserts that he had given such a body of teaching to the Corinthians, when he was with them. "I praise you, that ye remember me in all things, and keep the traditions, as I delivered them to you[8]." And specifically he reminds them, how he had taught them about the Holy Eucharist[9], and in much detail about our Lord's Resurrection[10], so that some few only were found who denied it[1].

---

[11] Acts xi. 26.
[3] Acts xviii. 18.
[6] Acts xx. 27—31.
[9] 1 Cor. xi. 23—26.
[1] Acts xv. 35.
[4] Acts xx. 31.
[7] Acts xxviii. 30, 31.
[10] 1 Cor. xv. 3—8.
[2] Acts xviii. 11.
[5] Acts xix. 8, 9.
[8] 1 Cor. xi. 2.
[1] Ib. 12.

f. Unless other doctrines than those contained in those elementary sermons to the unconverted were essential to salvation in those who can know them, it is inconceivable how S. John should sum up his Gospel, so full of doctrine, "These things are written, that ye might believe that Jesus is the Christ, the Son of God, and that, believing, ye might have life in His Name[2]." His Name surely, as He had spoken of Him in that Gospel, "Very God," and "for us and for our salvation, Very Man."

g. And yet even those doctrines selected by Bishop Moberly are not all contained in the letter of those sermons in the Acts. "The *incarnation and birth*" of the Son of God are related in the Gospels, they are not mentioned in the Acts. The descent of the Holy Ghost is mentioned oftentimes; His abiding "indwelling in the Church," or the souls of the faithful, is taught in the Gospels, is a prominent teaching of the Epistles, not of the Acts.

ii. Bishop Moberly, of course, understands the words, in which he has drawn up the original Gospel, in their fullest sense; for he says, "I accept and embrace with all my heart that exposition of faith in all its affirmative statements of doctrine[3]." By the Son of God, then, he means "God the Son," and by the Holy Ghost, the third Person in the Holy Trinity. But this being so, he includes, as essential teaching, the belief in the Holy Trinity and the Incarnation, which are the very doctrines guarded by those warning clauses of the Athanasian Creed. The word "Incarnation" itself contains all this doctrine, against which early heresy rebelled, that He Who was Very God, became, in the Virgin's womb, Very Man. His words, "atoning death upon the cross," have a more theological sound than the simpler, though equivalent terms of the Nicene Creed, "was crucified for us," or of the Athanasian, "suffered for our salvation," in which some acquiesce, who rebel against the word "atoning," "atonement."

[2] St. John xx. 31.   [3] App. p. 19.

But, then, on no principle can the statements of the Athanasian Creed, which are involved in these, and bound up in them, be relegated to another province, and *that* of fallibility. Had our Lord not been, equally with the Father, Uncreate, Infinite, Eternal, Almighty, Lord, co-equal with Him in His Godhead, inferior to Him as to His Manhood only, He had not been God. The Arian controversies only showed the hopelessness of trying to make out some middle term between God and a creature. "A second God," of which Arius spoke, involved Polytheism, or the worship of a creature. On the other hand, had our Lord not been "of the substance of His Mother" (which the Gnostics and Eutyches denied) "of a reasonable soul and human flesh subsisting" (which Apollinarius denied), God and Man without confusion of substance, He had not been Man. The Athanasian Creed contains not human though true developments of the Nicene Creed, but denials of falsehood, which would contradict and annul it. Why then make distinctions between those facts of the Gospel, which Bishop Moberly places under the word "faith," in his own human words, and those same facts as vindicated and cleared by the Church against the perversion of heretics? The Church, more in unison with the words of the Gospel, sets forth *that* belief as belief, not in any series of facts, but in the Holy Trinity and in our Lord Jesus Christ, "Very God, and for our salvation, Very Man," of our very nature, our Redeemer, and our Judge.

iii. The whole of Bishop Moberly's argument in favour of his distinction turns on the supposition that the word "baptized" includes every thing which in the Christian life follows after Baptism. But the word baptized [$\beta\alpha\pi\tau\iota\sigma\theta\epsilon\iota\varsigma$] by its very form, expresses a single act; nor do I know of any writer who has forced the word to mean any thing else. Faith and baptism are the entrance into the Christian life; and we pray for our newly-baptized infants that they "may lead the rest of their life according to this beginning." But to force into the one word "is baptized"—an act which takes place once for all, and which may not be repeated,

"Creeds, ordinances, chiefly the two Sacraments of the Gospel, with the rules and methods of administration to be determined by the Church, the powers left by the Lord in the Church, with their intelligible rules, their methods, their duly ordered and subordinated authorities"—

to force all this into the one word "baptized" is to do violence to language, and contrary to its laws. It is essential to Bishop Moberly's argument to force the Creeds into the word "baptized;" but how the Creeds, which express the one unchangeable faith, can belong to the word "baptized," and not to the word "believe," I cannot imagine. The faith, as stated at Nice, was (as Bishop Moberly knows) the same which was taught by the Apostles. They, at that time, must know better than we, what they received, or whether they added any thing. But it is the declaration of every Father, of every Council, that they added nothing new. "What they wrote down was no new discovery of theirs, but is the same as was taught by the Apostles [4]."

We know, from other words of our Lord, that in those who are baptized a living faith is required, a "faith which worketh by love," the keeping of God's commandments, perseverance to the end. Our Lord cannot by this brief formula, "He that believeth and is baptized shall be saved," mean to supersede His own words, "He that shall persevere unto the end, the same shall be saved." Belief is not a single act but a habit, a grace, a virtue, a living principle. The "observing all things whatsoever I have commanded you" (our Lord's words in S. Matthew [5]) are included in the word "believeth" in S. Mark,

[4] S. Ath. Conc. Arim. et Seleuc. § 5, p. 80, Oxf. Tr. See the like statements from Fathers and Councils, as given briefly in Dr. Pusey's sermon, "The Rule of Faith."

[5] Bp. Moberly makes a distinction between the word used by S. Matthew, "make disciples of" ($\mu\alpha\theta\eta\tau\epsilon\acute{\upsilon}\sigma\alpha\tau\epsilon$,) and that of S. Mark, " preach the Gospel to," ($\kappa\eta\rho\acute{\upsilon}\xi\alpha\tau\epsilon\ \tau\grave{o}\ \epsilon\grave{\upsilon}\alpha\gamma\gamma\acute{\epsilon}\lambda\iota o\nu$); but they differ no otherwise than that the word in S. Matthew expresses that that "preaching" should obtain its end of winning to Christ, those to whom the Gospel should be preached. Both

since the faith whereby a man shall be saved is a living faith. "Faith without works is dead." To depart from belief is apostasy; such become unbelievers; and whoever they shall be, fall under our Lord's sentence, although He alone knows who *they* are, who fall finally.

iv. It is, then, of little moment whether S. Bernard's distinction of the relative necessity of faith and baptism, is hinted in these words of our Lord, or no. For anyhow, as S. Bernard himself applies it [e], the word "is baptized," relates to the one act, whereby a person has been made a member of Christ. Our Lord speaks of that act in the first clause; "He that believes and is baptized shall be saved." In addition to the belief in Himself, our Lord requires the outward confession of that belief; whence S. Paul says, "With the heart man believeth

are united in the mention of those converted at Derbe. "Having preached the Gospel to (εὐαγγελισάμενοι) that city, and made many disciples (μαθητεύσαντες ἱκανοὺς), they returned, &c." (Acts xiv. 21). μαθητεύειν passively, is to be a disciple (S. Matt. xxvii. 57); actively, it is to make one a disciple (S. Matt. xxviii. 19. Acts l.c.), the same as μαθητὰς ποιεῖν (S. John iv. 21), "make disciples." The name itself, "disciple" (μαθητής), although occurring 250 times in the Gospels, and 30 times in the Acts as the title of Christians, "a disciple," "the disciples," disappears afterwards. It no where occurs in the Epistles.

[e] S. Bernard says:—"Consider whether when the Saviour said, 'He who believeth and is baptized shall be saved,' He did not carefully and of set purpose omit to repeat 'But he who is not baptized,' saying only, 'But he who believeth not, shall be condemned,' hinting that sometimes faith alone sufficeth to salvation, and without it nothing sufficeth.'" [Tract de Bapt. Opp. i. 629]. The argument does not turn on the mere omission of the word "baptized." For had it been simply added, it would have spoken, not of those who, believing, had yet not been baptized, but of those who not believing were not baptized. In the first clause, the subject is one and the same class of persons. "He who believeth and is baptized shall be saved." The words speak of two acts, one inward, the other outward, of the same persons. The meaning negatived by S. Bernard, could only have been introduced by an alteration of the construction, by which the repudiation of the inward act [faith] should be spoken of one class of persons, the omission of the outward act [baptism] of another. "Whosoever shall not believe, and whosoever shall not be baptized, shall be condemned." But anyhow, his observation does not yield the slightest support to Bishop Moberly, since it only relates to baptism received or neglected, not to any thing subsequent, whether of faith or life.

unto righteousness, and with the mouth confession is made unto salvation[7]." During those ages of persecution (and now, too, for those not born of Christian parents, Jews or Heathen) there must have often been a terrible temptation not to avow their belief, like those " chief rulers," of whom S. John says, " Many believed on Him, but because of the Pharisees they did not confess Him, lest they should be put out of the synagogue, for they loved the praise of men more than the praise of God[8]." Of such as these our Lord says, " Whosoever shall be ashamed of Me and of My words in this sinful and adulterous generation, of him also shall the Son of Man be ashamed when He cometh in the glory of His Father with the holy angels[9]."

In the second clause the mention of Baptism was superfluous, because, except in the case of Baptism in hypocrisy (such as that of Simon Magus), one who did not believe would obviously not be baptized. Nay, his being baptized would only bring additional guilt, as involving hypocrisy. Of course, there is no question as to the truth of what S. Bernard says, that they who believed, yet were not baptized, either through no fault of their own (as in the case of martyrdom), or through a repented fault (as of the delay of Baptism and sudden death supervening) would be accepted by God. Both come under the general law, that God, in His mercy, accepts the will for the deed. S. Bernard would have been not a little startled to find his words, in which he said that " faith " might in some cases " suffice to salvation," enlisted in behalf on the surmise that the faith, as rehearsed in the Creeds, is not necessary in those who could have it.

v. Bp. Moberly qualifies our blessed Lord's words, " He that believeth not shall be condemned," by referring the whole subject to the omniscience of God. He lays down very definitely certain points, the Incarnation and Birth of the Son of God, His Atoning Death upon the Cross, and other articles of the Creed, as included in that Gospel message, which " when it is preached to a man he must believe or not believe ;" but he says,

---

[7] Rom. x. 10.   [8] S. John xii. 42, 43.   [9] Mark viii. 38.

man cannot tell what is, or what is not, "real and acceptable belief or unbelief."

"When the Gospel facts are duly published, according to our Lord's command, man must either believe or disbelieve, and, according as he does one or the other, he is, *pro tanto*, in the condition of assured salvation or the opposite. I wish to insist upon this point. The whole sphere of fitness or unfitness for salvation, so far as this first and chief condition is concerned, must needs be in the hands and in the judgment of the all-seeing God alone."

But our Lord's words, "He that believeth not shall be condemned," are just as distinct as those with which the Athanasian Creed closes; "This is the Catholic faith, which, except a man believe faithfully, he cannot be saved." Bishop Moberly acknowledges that an universal proposition must, in its application, be modified by, or according to, the circumstances of each. This is acknowledged in human law universally. The law lays down the punishment upon murder or manslaughter. Human law takes into account the circumstances which exempt any given case from being either murder or manslaughter, and places it either under the milder of the two, or under the class of "justifiable homicide." It takes account of motives, i.e. moral grounds, in weighing the character of a deed, upon which the heaviest temporal penalty of Divine or human law rests. There is scarcely a general proposition, upon any subject; there is even scarcely a general statement upon religion which does not require such modification, and which, when applied to individual cases, does not receive it at the hands of the common sense of mankind. The Sermon upon the Mount, with its simple, strong lawgiving upon large moral subjects, its code of Christian morals, is practically modified in its application to individual cases. A rigid unmodified interpretation, which might be Christian humility in one case, might be provocative in another.

I should myself far extend the exemptions which Bishop Moberly suggests in regard to that solemn admonition of our Lord, "He that believeth not shall be condemned." And I trust, that Bishop Moberly will himself, on further thought, see the necessity of such an extension; else I think that he throws a stumbling-block in the way of those, as yet outside the Gospel, who are feeling their way back to it. At present he suggests as such, " the approaches with tears and inward consciousness of feeble faith," but " *with their best*," " the heart and disposition of belief, even though the intellectual conviction and sense of assurance be imperfect [1]," or " eagerness to cling to Him though mingled with inaccuracy of conception." As to such cases as these, I could not even imagine a doubt, that they would be accepted, since they are supposed to come to Him " with their best." Sin being in the will, one could not doubt as to those whose will is supposed to be right. He has said, " Whoso cometh unto Me, I will in no wise cast out." One could not doubt of His receiving those who " with an honest and true heart" came to Him, however imperfect their convictions. For myself, I do not doubt that Divine mercy will be extended very far beyond these limits, and that Bishop Moberly is wrong, alike as to the strictness of the limits which he draws as to those who have refused the faith altogether, and as to the grounds upon which he believes that the sentence will be relaxed to many whose faith is unsound. I do *not* believe that all " unbelief is distinctly and hopelessly condemned." In any case, I believe, that with regard to individuals, the ground of rejection will lie, not in the outward fact of unbelief, whether in the Gospel as a whole, or in truths which form an integral part of the Gospel, but in the heart and in some perversity of will, of which God alone is the Judge.

But, then, since the like exceptions are made in all legislation, Divine and human, since, even when there is no doubt as to the fact and the guilt, even human justice recognizes extenuating circumstances, and " recommends to mercy" those whom the strict sentence of the law condemns to death, since our Lord's

---

[1] Bp. Moberly, App. p. 36. See above, Sermon, p. 37 sqq.

words, "He that believeth not shall be condemned," are the words of our Judge, and must abide in their everlasting truth, yet we doubt not, that He will, perhaps, to a multitude which no man can number, own as His redeemed, those who knew Him not as their Redeemer, why is it to be a ground of exception to the warning words of the Athanasian Creed, which are simply an application of them, that they lay down a general law in absolute words, leaving all individual cases to be decided by our Judge's Omniscience and Almighty Love?

I much wish that Bp. Moberly had set himself, with that clearness which was once his characteristic, to look in the face our Lord's words, "He that believeth not shall be condemned," and to consider what explanation they must (in common with so many other general declarations of Holy Scripture) receive in regard to individuals, if we are not to understand, that our Lord meant to declare that every individual would perish, to whom the Gospel has been or shall be preached, and he has not, or shall not receive it. If he does not think this, he will have no difficulty in adapting that explanation to the Athanasian Creed. He says:—

"If the damnatory clauses [I regret to see Bishop Moberly adopting the coarse term of their opponents] are to be understood in what many people regard as their understood grammatical and literal sense, that is, as pronouncing the eternal condemnation of all those who *under any circumstances* do not accept and believe the entire frame of Divine doctrine declared in this Creed, I, for one, do not believe them."

Notwithstanding some assertions which look the contrary way, I think that Bp. Moberly would be startled, if any one were to adapt his sentence to our Lord's words:—

"If the sentence, pronounced by our Lord, 'He that believeth not shall be condemned,' is to be understood in what many people regard as its understood grammatical and literal sense, that is, as pronouncing the eternal condemnation of all those who, *under any circumstances,* do not accept the Gospel message preached unto them, I——"

I do not believe that such *is* the literal meaning either of our Lord's words in this or other like places, or of the Athanasian

Creed, which is framed upon them. I believe that they both mean exactly the same; that in both a general principle is enunciated, that "faith in God, as He Is and as He has declared Himself, Three Divine Persons, but One God, and in our Lord Jesus Christ, One God with the Father, and Man, of our substance, Who died for our sins," is necessary to salvation in all who can have it; but that the application of this principle lies with Him, Whose attributes are "mercy and judgment," but with Whom, wherever it is possible, "mercy triumpheth over judgment."

In the first quarter of this century we used to hear of the "perishing heathen" as an argument for missions. I can hardly conceive any thing which should make missionary labour so oppressive, as the thought that one was aggravating the condition of those who, through one's own imperfection in preaching the Gospel, should fail to receive it. And, in fact, there is probably no preaching of the Gospel now, which does not involve the doctrines of the Athanasian Creed, seeing that the distinctive part of it is the clear exposition of the belief in God as He Is, Father, Son, and Holy Ghost, and in our Lord Jesus Christ, Very God, and for us and our salvation, become Very Man.

From the way in which the attack upon the Athanasian Creed has been carried on, I do not think that the subject of an "explanatory note" has really been entertained. The assailants of the Creed have, of course, dismissed it, wishing to get rid of the Creed altogether; the maintainers of the Creed have been shy of it, fearing that it would be interpreted as an acknowledgment, that the Creed stood in need of such an explanation, and so that its recommendation would be turned into an argument against the Creed. The way in which the note suggested by the Oxford Divinity Professors, as one to which we saw no objection, was misinterpreted, certainly countenanced those fears. The Professors drew up that formula, on my representation, that, having been requested to furnish "such a note as I could acquiesce in," I had engaged to do it, after conference with them. They consented, some of them rather reluctantly. It was argued in Convocation, that by sending this explanatory note, we ourselves acknowledged the need of one, and, consequently, the obscurity of the Creed. "These Professors," it was argued, "acknowledge the obscurity of these clauses, in that they send an explanation of them. If so, they virtually acknowledge their unfitness for use." As though every Creed, nay many prayers, or our Catechism, or Holy Scripture, do not require to be explained to the uninstructed.

Two chief modes of explanation have been adopted hitherto; the one, that of the Ritual Commissioners declaring what class of persons are *not* included under its—or rather our Lord's—sentence against those who " believe not ;" the other declaring what class of persons alone *are* included under it. The Oxford Professors adopted the negative form. For myself, I should have preferred to combine both, that " the clauses apply to those only, who, out of a perverse will reject the faith contained in that Creed, not to those who, from involuntary ignorance or invincible prejudice, do not receive it."

The explanation, "involuntary ignorance and invincible prejudice," is but a popular substitution for the known theological term, "invincible ignorance." Bishop Moberly argues against it, partly from a sense which he affixes to the word "invincible," viz. that " which *we* cannot conquer [2]." The theological meaning is, "which *the individual himself* cannot conquer." Its chief domain is in hereditary error, which a person has imbibed as truth, from the teaching of his parents, his educators, his ministers of irreligion or error, whom he believes to be ministers of religion and of truth.

Bishop Moberly thinks it almost inconceivable that " there should be prejudices conquerable which cannot be conquered [3]."

[2] "Does not this exception of unconquerable prejudice go the length of excepting every body whose prejudice *we* cannot conquer ?"—App. p. 27.

[3] " If there be any man—heathen, Jew, heretic, apostate—who holds fast

I can hardly imagine any one conversant with the prejudices of those brought up in hereditary error, who cannot conceive it. If not, the blame and guilt as to *all* error, must belong either to those who have the truth or those who have it not. Either *we*, through our own fault or guilt, do not teach the truth so as to conquer *their* prejudices, or *they*, through their own fault or guilt, do not use those means (whatever they be), by which, through God's grace, they should be conquered. I do not believe the alternative to be necessary. I believe that there is very much prejudice, which is inculpable. The very adoption of the term "invincible ignorance" implies that this is the opinion of the greatest part of the Christian world. Who can imagine that the prejudice of all the large Nestorian or Jacobite communities is vincible, i.e. that they all are faulty, if they do not abandon the hereditary prejudices of 1400 years?

Bishop Moberly excepts equally to the expression of "*involuntary* ignorance." I should myself have preferred "inculpable ignorance," i.e. ignorance which did not arise in the individual's own fault, or which he might not, had he willed, have removed. But the term "involuntary ignorance" comes to the same. Sin and guilt lie in the will. A person may surely not be at pains to know the truth, from contempt of it, or indifference to it, or from being absorbed in things of this world, or because acknowledgment of the truth would involve consequences, from which he shrinks. He might know it and does not. Bishop Moberly says truly :—

"I believe that no human analysis of ignorance can define with any accuracy the limits within and without which God, in His omniscience, will determine the fact of innocence or guilt in ignorance."—App. p. 29.

Truly. Nor have we attempted it. The Searcher of hearts alone can tell, in *whom* prejudice is invincible or ignorance

his prejudice against the Catholic faith, and *refuses to allow it to be conquered* in argument, does he not escape under this unlimited amnesty? Who is there, or who can there be, who does not escape under it. Except such (if it be conceivable that there are such) as entertain prejudices 'conquerable,' but not to be conquered?"—App. pp. 27, 28.

Appendix. 77

involuntary. Or, if we use the Theological term, "invincible ignorance," He alone knows in what cases the ignorance might be overcome. Or if (as being more popular) we use the term "inculpable ignorance," He is the Judge, what ignorance is culpable, what inculpable. Or if we said, "those only would be condemned who through perversity of will reject the truth unto the end," we condemn no one, but affirm only what character of mind alone He would reject.

A formula might perhaps commend itself, which should draw attention to the fact, that the Church never ventures to anticipate the final judgment of God, but leaves all to the All-merciful Judge, Who alone knoweth the secrets of all hearts, and hath compassion on the works of His Hands, whom He hath redeemed with His Precious Blood, if only they do not, even in their last hour, reject Him. Since, then, it has been a principle with the Church, not to condemn individuals, it ought not to be thought by any, that in this Creed she has departed from her universal rule. Perhaps such a formula might fall in with one mentioned by Bp. Moberly, as, on the whole, that with which he is least dissatisfied, and which he even thinks "would, as a temporary expedient, be useful," although only "as preparing the way for[4]" what he believes to be "the only real remedy," the extirpation of the clauses by a "Pan-Anglican Synod[5]." The note might perhaps run somehow thus[6]:—

"When it is variously declared in the Athanasian Creed, that belief in the truths contained therein is necessary to salvation, such declarations are to be understood in like manner as the sayings of our Lord Jesus Christ

---

[4] App. p. 52.

[5] I know not whether Bishop Moberly contemplates that if the Anglican Bishops were to force upon their Communion such a vital change, against the protests of many, doubtless, of their own order, and against a continually increasing voice of her Priests, for such an act a majority of such a Synod would suffice, if such could be obtained. It would be not a little inconsistent, after all the strictures on the Vatican Council for proceeding by a majority.

[6] The formula suggested to Bp. Moberly is that "the damnatory clauses are no otherwise to be understood than as the general sentences of God's wrath are generally set forth to us in Holy Scripture."

concerning belief or unbelief in Himself, namely, as proclaiming the rule of God's dealings with those to whom salvation is offered. No sentence of the Creed may be rightly applied by men to any one human soul; since the Church of herself never affirms the certain perdition of any man, but leaves all such judgment to the Searcher of hearts, Who discerneth unerringly between sinful rejection of any truth revealed by Himself, and blindness which, for whatever cause, is not sinful, and who will at the Great Day pronounce accordingly."

Bishop Moberly expresses with energy his adherence to the whole faith set forth in the Athanasian Creed. He says [7];

"I accept and embrace with all my heart that Exposition of Faith in all its affirmative statements of doctrine. In its clear, strong, incisive words; in its distinct definitions; in its repetitions (as some consider them, but which I regard either as statements in necessary detail, which have been first made in a general form); in every word of the affirmative doctrinal declarations respecting the Holy Trinity and the Incarnation of our Lord and Saviour Jesus Christ, I regard it as a document of inestimable value, and one which ought to hold its place in the public worship of Almighty God."

But, so believing himself, he seems to lay down two, as it seems to me, inconsistent grounds, why it should not be declared that the belief therein declared is essential to salvation:—

1. That it *is* a Creed, and that Creeds belong to human agency and so to human fallibility. His whole argument turns on the contrast of what he calls, "two spheres," the one, "the Gospel facts," "published according to our Lord's commands [8];" the other comprises, according to him, the whole office of the Church consequent upon the reception of those facts by a living faith. The "second sphere" is that of the Church in which he specifies the Creeds [9].

"Here it is plain that we pass at once into another sphere. Now we have to do with men; with their agency, their administration, and, of consequence, with their judgment. We enter, so to speak, into the domain of the visible Church. They whose hearts have been opened to give ear to the good Tidings and believe in Christ, have now to pass under the teaching of the Church, and to be made disciples into the Holy Name" [of the Trinity, the Father, the Son, and the Holy Ghost, into which they were, by Christ's command, baptized].

---

[7] Appendix, pp. 19, 20.   [8] Sermon, pp. 5—10.
[9] Sermon, p. 12.

Appendix. 79

"Then come in *Creeds*, the due and orderly development of the original baptismal formula, enlarged in after ages to meet and overthrow the perverse inventions of heresy."

The ground why Creeds should not be guarded by declaration that they are necessary to salvation, he lays down thus;

"In the Lord's words, regarding the first sphere [viz. the Gospel-facts], though they are perfectly general, there is no limitation. It is undoubtedly true that ὁ ἀπιστήσας κατακριθήσεται [He that believeth not shall be condemned]. But when a limitation is suggested to the words of the Creed, 'Which faith except every one do keep whole and undefiled without doubt he shall perish everlastingly;' the necessity of the limitation arises, not from the general nature of general statements, but from the fact that the fallibility of man enters into and is mixed with the authority of the doctrinal clauses, to which these solemn sanctions are appended[1]."

In other words, they are *not* "certain truth," for "the fallibility of man enters into them and is mixed with their authority." This seems to me to cut at the root of all Creeds and of all definite faith. I cannot imagine how one could recite to Almighty God what one did not know to be certain truth. A doubt as to its truth would canker our faith, and make our tongue falter. The doubts which Bishop Moberly suggests would penetrate the Nicene Creed equally with the Athanasian, the Apostles' equally with the Nicene. Creeds are to be somehow mixed with human fallibility. Where does it lie? Not in any one statement, but throughout, because it is human. From the beginning to the end, from the "I believe in God, the Father Almighty" down to "the life everlasting," all is to be uncertain. I see not how the Church is "the pillar and ground of the truth[2]," if even its Creeds are not to be exempt from liability to error. Bishop Moberly would, if I followed him, land me in an utter maze of scepticism. I pray that he may not lead thither any who follow out his thoughts.

2. This whole principle (that of the whole Sermon and Appendix applies equally to all Creeds. Elsewhere Bishop Moberly makes a distinction between the Nicene and the Athanasian. He asks,

[1] Page 41.   [2] 1 Tim. iii. 15.

"What degree or sort of assent is requisite, in order to give any decrees or determinations of the Church that quasi-infallibility, that assurance of being right and true, that confident certainty of proceeding from the inspiration of the Holy Spirit, which carries with it full authority on the consciences of dutiful Churchmen? We have always been taught that when a grave matter has been debated and decided in Œcumenical Council with prayer for the help of the Holy Spirit, and when, retrospectively, the general voice of the Church, clerical and lay, has accepted and sanctioned such determinations, then the consent is so complete, as to be really binding upon the consciences of dutiful Church people[3]."

But again the question arises, what is involved in being "binding upon the consciences of dutiful people?" This would be true of any decree of the universal Church. The Council of Nice made a decree about the time of keeping Easter; the whole Church obeyed and all disputings ceased. When the question of appeals to Rome was brought, in S. Augustine's time, before a Council of all Africa, "the whole Council said, 'All things which have been enacted in the Council of Nice are accepted by us all.'" A legate echoed, "What has been enacted in the Nicene Council may not in any way be violated by any[4]." The decrees even of a particular Church are binding on the consciences of its members, to obey them. The question is not as to our consciences, but as to the "certain truth" of that which is set forth to us as "the faith." The Council of Nice itself marked the distinction, as is impressed by S. Athanasius who was present at it.

"They wrote concerning the Easter, 'It seemeth good as follows,' for it did seem good that there should be a general compliance; but about the faith they wrote not, 'It seemeth good,' but, 'Thus believes the Catholic Church;' and thereupon they confessed how the faith lay, in order to shew that their own statements were not novel, but Apostolical; and what they wrote down was no discovery of theirs, but is the same as was taught by the Apostles[5]."

The faith in the Nicene Creed is (the Fathers of Nice claim), that which had descended from the Apostles to them, that

---

[3] Appendix, pp. 42, 43.
[4] Cod. Eccl. Afr. vii. p. 159, Ed. Bruns.
[5] Conc. Arim. Seleuc. n. 7; Treatises against Arianism, p. 80, Oxf. Tr.

which the Apostles preached. If it is the same, "cadit quæstio." The Nicene Fathers, gathered from the whole world, declared that it *was* the same; and,—following the example of S. Paul, who, full of love and of the Holy Ghost as he was, said, "If any man love not the Lord Jesus Christ, let him be Anathema Maranatha[6],' and, "though we, or an Angel from heaven, preach any other Gospel unto you than that which we have preached unto you, let him be accursed: as we said before, so now I say again, If any man preach any other Gospel unto you, than that which we have preached unto you, let him be accursed[7],"— annexed anathemas to it.

Did then Arius or the Council of Nice, or both, teach another Gospel? Bishop Moberly declares those "Gospel facts," which he has put in his human words, to be the original Gospel. To these, he says, "our Lord's words apply without limitation." Then to his compendium it might be added, "This he who believeth not shall be condemned." If the Council of Nice taught and confessed the self-same Gospel which the Apostles preached, then the same solemn sanction applies to both. If not, it would itself have fallen under the Apostle's Anathema.

Bishop Moberly seems to me to have confused words with things. He could not and does not doubt that when S. Peter said in his preaching, "the God of our fathers has glorified His Son Jesus[8]," "God, having raised up His Son Jesus," and when S. Paul "preached Christ in the synagogues, that He is the Son of God[9]," they meant to assert His Divine Nature, that He is "His own Son[1]," "God of God, Very God of Very God[2]." Bishop Moberly himself sets down "the Incarnation of our Lord Jesus Christ" as one of those primal "Gospel facts:" he must include in them the fact of the existence of the All-Holy Trinity, Father, Son, and Holy Ghost, One God.

But these are the very truths, so dwelt upon in the Athanasian

---

[6] 1 Cor. xvi. 22.
[8] Acts iii. 13, 26.
[1] Rom. viii. 3, 32.

[7] Gal. i. 8, 9.
[9] Ibid. ix. 20.
[2] Nicene Creed.

Creed. No statement of it could be denied, either as to the Holy Trinity, or the Incarnation, which would leave the Being of God or the Person of our Lord the same. It clears those doctrines most lustrously to our minds; it explains to us what might be difficulties in our Lord's own words; it adds nothing which does not lie in the Nicene Creed.

What Bishop Moberly pleads against it, as issuing from no Council[3], would hold equally against the Apostles' Creed. Of it, equally, "we do not know by whom it was drawn, or when or where." For although its substantial identity every where makes it probable that it came from the Apostles themselves, we have only the probability of the case and tradition in support of this belief. The Apostles' and the Athanasian Creeds have alike been received into the public service of the Western Church: the Athanasian Creed has received the distinct approval of the Eastern Church; and so has the authority of the whole Church, which every where, although separately, has borne and bears witness to the truth[4].

Bishop Moberly proposes and anticipates that a Synod of the Bishops of the English Communion should and would remove the "warning clauses," including, of course, the clauses " He therefore that would be saved, let him thus think of the Trinity," and " Furthermore it is necessary to everlasting salvation, that he also believe rightly the Incarnation of our Lord Jesus Christ." For these, although in varying terms, express exactly the same as those on which the opponents of the Creed most dwell. For to say that " it is *necessary* to everlasting salvation to believe rightly " is, of course, identical with

---

[3] Appendix, p. 43.

[4] The Rev. G. Williams tells me:—1. That in a kind of Appendix to the Horologium, in which the Athanasian Creed is printed, it is stated to be "consonant with the doctrine of the Orthodox Church." 2. In the Σύνοψις Ἱερά, being an abbreviation of "the Hours," it is described (with the rest of the contents on the title-page) as " useful to each Christian." 3. Macarius, a Russian Divine of repute, places the Athanasian Creed among "the expositions of the faith, which, though not examined and expressly approved by the Councils, are yet *received* by the whole Catholic Church."

saying that, "unless he believe it, he cannot be saved." To say that food is necessary to support our bodily life, is all one with saying, unless a man take food he will die. But, apart from the question what right a particular Church has to alter a Creed sanctioned by the Universal Church, the English Church would, by removing these clauses, assert in a most emphatic way, and teach its people, that it did *not* believe that a right faith in the Holy Trinity or the Incarnation of our Lord Jesus Christ is necessary to salvation[5]. For, if she believes them to be necessary, she would not remove from the Creed the declaration that they are so. But, if these were not necessary, what else could be? For one who disbelieves in the Holy Trinity believes in a different God. He who does not "believe rightly the Incarnation" does (as the instances of Nestorius, Eutyches, and the rest have shown) not believe in the Incarnation at all. If any believe not the Incarnation, neither can he believe rightly what Bishop Moberly selects as necessary to be

[5] An eminent layman has said that "the Church of England would, notwithstanding the removal of the Creed, retain the same belief in the Holy Trinity so long as it should retain the opening prayers of the Litany." But how long would this be? Why should it retain them, if it should no longer think them "necessary to salvation"? It would be hard to believe that the doctrine was revealed at all; for why should God reveal such a mystery as to Himself, if it were unnecessary for us to believe it?

The change would express a disbelief, which would leave those who should acquiesce in it, no standing ground for asserting any other truth to be essential to Christianity, or to our salvation as Christians. Bishop Moberly has already suggested an alteration in the Nicene Creed which would change our belief as to the Being of God. The Council of Florence rightly stated that the two modes of expression, "the Procession of the Holy Ghost from the Father and the Son," and "the Procession of the Holy Ghost from the Father through the Son," mean the same. Both East and West hold the same faith, although, since the Satanic acuteness of Photius, the Greeks have learnt to think a mode of expression familiar to their forefathers heretical. Were the Church of England to reject the "Filioque," I have no doubt that it would become heretical in this also. For it has no tradition, like that of the Greeks, to uphold its faith, and the effacing of this expression of our belief would alter our belief itself. It would come to believe in God as existing in a different way from that in which He does exist, i. e. it would believe in a different God.

believed, "the Atoning Death upon the Cross;" if he believe not rightly the doctrine of the Trinity, neither can he believe "the descent of the Holy Ghost upon the Church," since he would not believe that there *is* any Holy Ghost. The Church of England would become a mere aggregate of individuals, who believed, every one, what seemed good in his own eyes, a sand-hill with no internal coherence. More than this, it would come under our Lord's heavy words upon those, who, " in an adulterous and sinful generation," should be " ashamed of Him and His words:" it would, by denying His words, have denied Himself; and, disowning Him, would be disowned by Him.

www.ingramcontent.com/pod-product-compliance
Lightning Source LLC
Chambersburg PA
CBHW031605110426
42742CB00037B/1263